A character sketch of the author by Leo Hershfield

The Arts of the Sailor

Knotting, Splicing and Ropework

HERVEY GARRETT SMITH

ILLUSTRATED BY THE AUTHOR

DOVER PUBLICATIONS, INC.

NEW YORK

Published in Canada by General Publishing Company, Ltd., 30 Lesmill Road, Don Mills, Toronto, Ontario.
Published in the United Kingdom by Constable and Company, Ltd.

This Dover edition, first published in 1990, is an unabridged republication of the work originally published as *The Arts of the Sailor* in 1953 by D. Van Nostrand Company, Inc., New York.

Manufactured in the United States of America
Dover Publications, Inc., 31 East 2nd Street, Mineola, N.Y. 11501

Library of Congress Cataloging-in-Publication Data

Smith, Hervey Garrett.
     The arts of the sailor : knotting, splicing, and ropework / Hervey Garrett Smith.
          p.   cm.
     Reprint. Originally published: New York : Van Nostrand, 1953.
     ISBN 0-486-26440-8
     1. Marline spike seamanship.   2. Yachts and yachting.   I. Title.
VM531.S57   1990
623.88′82—dc20   90-3262
                                                                       CIP

Preface

The arts of the sailor have been defined as "a collection of related skills employed in the rigging, working and maintenance of a ship." They partake variously of the craft of the rigger, the sailmaker and the able-bodied seaman, and are as old as the age of sail.

Born of necessity and nurtured through hundreds of years, they reached the highest point of their development in the early part of the nineteenth century, in the heyday of the Yankee whaleman. By mid-century the decline was well underway, and with the passing of the merchant sailing ship the rope-and-canvas sailor was headed for oblivion, cast adrift on a mechanized sea and master of an almost obsolete art.

Almost, but not quite. There remained the increasingly numerous yachts, sailing the same seas and borne by the same winds, and dependent upon the same ancient skills for their rigging, handling and maintenance; the sailor's arts were as necessary to the man who sailed for pleasure as they were to the professional. Today, yachtsmen all over the world are perpetuating these traditional skills of the romantic era of sail which are their rightful heritage.

But proficiency in these arts is hard come by. The yachtsman perforce acquires much of his knowledge piecemeal, by personal observation and helpful advice from more experienced friends. Much of this information may be found in books, but generally it is buried amidst extraneous material that is of little or no value in modern yachting as we know it today. The best existing sources suffer alike in that they are too comprehensive, and in the attempt to cover everything they are of little use to the man with some specific problem relating to the maintenance and operation of a small boat. Rarely does he have the time or the sustained interest for extensive research, and the scope of his learning is therefore largely a matter of chance—inadequate and incomplete.

In this book will be found all of the skills involving rope and canvas that are required by the average boat owner, and in the selection of material I have endeavoured to include only such subjects as are immediately and continually useful. It is intended to be used as a handbook—to be kept aboard the boat for ready reference as the need arises. Taken as a whole, it constitutes a complete course of instruction in the basic arts of the sailor as practiced today.

In my own experience, such knowledge as I possess was acquired with difficulty, involving the expenditure of considerable time and effort that was often hard to justify. But in the final analysis, the pleasures that I have derived from the practice of these skills more than compensate for the endeavour. With this in mind it is my sincere hope that this book will make the going a little smoother for others, and that they will experience the same lasting enjoyment that has been mine.

The urge to share one's experience stirs within the

breast of many men, and I am no exception; therefore I shall always be a self-appointed missionary, carrying the light to the dark places and preaching the gospel according to Matthew Walker.

Sayville, Long Island   H{ERVEY} G{ARRETT} S{MITH}
June, 1953

Contents

CONTENTS

The Anatomy of Rope and Cordage

Upon acquiring his first boat the embryo yachtsman discovers that its use is going to involve intimate, personal contact with rope and cordage, and to a far greater extent than he anticipated. He learns that rope has an infinite number of applications in which he will be called upon to employ diverse knots, bends, hitches and splices. It must be secured to a variety of objects, temporarily or permanently, withstand all manner of stresses and strains and withal perform efficiently and safely at all times. In short, rope has suddenly assumed an importance that he cannot ignore, and, if he is an average landsman, is not prepared to cope with.

To put rope to work intelligently, and to make the most of its amazing versatility calls for something more than the ability to tie a simple knot or hitch. When you consider that the same rope which might some day save your life can just as efficiently kill or maim, it should be evident that a thorough understanding of its structural characteristics is vitally important.

Suppose we unlay a section of half-inch, common Manila rope to examine its component parts and the nature of its construction. You will observe that the three strands are *right-laid*, that is they spiral around the rope to the right, or clockwise. Each strand is composed of seven individual yarns or threads which are *left-laid*, or twisted counter-clockwise. Right there is the reason rope constantly holds its form and resists any tendency to unlay. If you grasp a rope with your two hands a couple of inches apart and try to unlay it or separate the strands you will notice that a quarter of a turn is about all you can comfortably gain. In trying to untwist the rope you were actually attempting to lay up the yarns more tightly.

Each yarn is composed of a group of natural fibers twisted together *right-handed,* and careful examination will disclose that despite the spiral construction of rope, every fiber of it runs constantly *straight* in the direction that the rope lies. That is the secret of its strength, and an important factor limiting the amount of stretch.

Such is the simple manner in which rope is put together—fibers spun or twisted right-handed into yarns, yarns laid up left-handed into strands, and the strands right-laid to form the finished rope. But elementary though it may seem, it is imperative that it be firmly fixed in your mind if you would master the arts of the sailor, for the natural lay of the parts must be preserved at all times. Any loosening or tightening of the normal "twist" of the strands or yarns greatly reduces the strength of the rope and shortens its life. In splicing and numerous other operations where it is necessary to unlay the rope and disarrange the strands, you must be able to restore it to its original lay, so that every yarn bears an equal share of the load. All too many otherwise-proficient yachtsmen ignore or forget this simple fundamental when they turn in a splice, and as a result you find one strand overstrained and the other two inert.

The fibers of Manila rope are inherently wiry and stiff; thus it has a natural tendency to hold its lay and is relatively easy to work with. At the other extreme is cotton rope, in which the fibers are soft and limp. When you cut cotton rope it instantly unlays for a considerable distance and falls apart at the touch. Once unlaid, it resists every attempt to restore its original form and therefore is somewhat difficult to splice.

Rope gains in strength when it becomes wet because the water softens the fibers and "fairs up" the lay. Likewise knots, bends, and hitches tighten up and are much stronger when wet. In fact, many knots and hitches are unsuited for use at sea because they get so tight when wet that it is almost impossible to untie them, and there are times when this fault could have tragic consequences.

Wet rope also shrinks. When a dry rope, stretched taut and secured at each end, becomes wet terrific strains are set up and something has to give. One of two things inevitably happens—either the part to which it is attached tears loose or the rope is stretched beyond its recovery limit and is permanently damaged. Rope that has become so attenuated and has lost much of its twist is called "long-jawed." *Never* leave a dry rope set up taut, be it sheet, halyard or dock line, for the first shower to wet it can destroy much of its usefulness.

The two greatest enemies of rope are friction and rot—both of which can be combatted by proper care and handling. Internal friction, the constant rubbing together of the fibers, can result from the use of blocks with sheaves of too small a diameter, or conversely, too large a rope for the block. External friction, which chafes and cuts the surface fibers, can be caused by many things. Dragging rope along the ground or over sharp surfaces, failure to apply chafing gear, improper "lead" of running rigging and use of cleats too small for the size of rope used—all help in the rapid depreciation of rope. Kinks and snarls are also enemies, and the prudent sailor constantly overhauls his rope by coiling it down neatly so it is ever ready to run free. Never put a strain on a rope that is kinked or whose normal lay has been distorted.

Rot is caused by a fungus which thrives on dampness. Immersion in sea-water leaves the rope impregnated with salt, which continually absorbs moisture from the air and makes it difficult to entirely prevent rot from starting. However, you can delay its progress by keeping your rope as dry as possible, well aired and out of the sun. Never put rope below deck when wet, and store only where it is well ventilated. An occasional bath in fresh water will remove salt, keep rope soft and pleasant to handle, and prolong its life.

There are a number of excellent rope preservatives available which have gained considerable popularity, particularly among commercial fishermen, who use them for the prevention of rot in nets and rope. Rope so treated is inclined to be somewhat sticky and therefore not too desirable for sheets and halyards; but for preserving mooring and anchor cables which are continuously wet I can heartily recommend the treatment. Six years after applying one of these preservatives my cables show no sign of rot or "powdering," and the initial stickiness has long since disappeared.

In spite of every care taken to prolong its life, there comes a time when rope should be replaced. Normal wear, exposure to the elements, and old age take their toll and it can no longer be trusted. To determine just when that point has been reached you must recognize the signs when they appear, and that means careful, periodic inspection. The best indication is the condition of the fibers. Those on the surface are broken, and the rope has a hairy look. Unlay a strand and pull out a fiber. Notice that it is only a few inches long, whereas it was probably ten or twelve feet long when the rope was new. The inside fibers will be matted and powdery, have a lifeless, gray look and some will be broken. The rope will have completely lost its original wiry springiness, and no elasticity remains whatsoever. Notice how much smaller its diameter is compared to what it was when new—three-eighths rope has probably become five-sixteenths—and it is decidedly long-jawed. It should be obvious that the time to replace rope is *before* this point has been reached rather than after it has parted in use.

In the foregoing discussion the term "rope" has been used in its broader, more generic sense. But there are many kinds of rope, each with its own characteristics, and none universally suitable for every use. There are also the "small stuff," light lines and seizing material under the general heading of *cordage,* each with specified uses and having its own peculiarities. To choose the right one for the job in hand, and to use it intelligently, you must have a basic understanding of the various materials at your command. To that end I suggest we have a look at them, see where they may be used, and learn why they act the way they do.

Manila

The fibers used in the manufacture of Manila rope come from a plant called "abaca" grown in the Philippines. These fibers run anywhere from three to ten or twelve feet in length, the longest going into only the finest quality of rope. They are graded not only for length, but also for uniformity in size. In their raw state Manila fibers contain a natural oil, and more oil is added when the rope is manufactured. These oils leach away gradually through exposure to the elements, and deprived of their necessary lubrication, the fibers deteriorate rapidly.

There is more Manila rope used in the world today than any other kind, and the chances are that you will be depending upon it most of the time you are afloat. Certain it is that Manila is the most versatile of all, and by and large the most dependable of all rope materials, but you *must* use careful judgment in its selection. There are many grades of Manila, and no two manufacturers seem to grade their rope in the same manner.

Low grade, poor quality rope is easy to recognize, and has no place on a well-found yacht. It is extremely hairy and coarse, the ends of its short fibers sticking out everywhere throughout its length. Unlay a strand and you will notice that the fibers vary greatly in size, and many are looped, kinked and snarled. Some of the yarns are larger than others, bunchy and gouty, and the lay of the rope lacks uniformity. Such rope is dangerous and unreliable. Its strength is unpredictable and its elasticity is an unknown factor.

The best quality of Manila obtainable is the grade known as "Yacht Rope," and only the very finest of fibers and workmanship go into its construction. Its most noticeable characteristics are the perfect uniformity of its lay, and the absence of protruding fiber ends. It is slick and smooth to handle, reeves through blocks with a minimum of friction, and is extremely long-lived. When unlaid, you will find that every yarn is almost identical, the long fibers are uniform in size and very few ends are visible. The strands are mechanically perfect throughout the rope and have a decidedly sculptured appearance.

Because of the high quality of the fiber and the precision with which it is laid, inner friction is reduced to a minimum and its strength is a constant factor, from one end of the coil to the other. Truly it is a superior product, and hence it commands a considerably higher price than the common grades.

Only slightly below "Yacht Rope" in quality is the grade known as "Bolt Rope." With the same long-fiber construction, it has a slightly harder lay, and like "Yacht Rope," is available in both 3 and 4 strands. After many years of experience in its use I am convinced that 4-strand "Bolt Rope" is unequaled for sheets. Here the rope is constantly moving through the blocks, alternately trimmed under strain and slacked off at high speed. Sheets must run freely without kinking, withstand severe inner friction, and be easy on the hands.

4-strand "Bolt Rope" does all of these with ease, and what is more, resists wear and chafe to a marked degree.

One word of caution . . . 4-strand rope is often made with an inner "heart" yarn, or core, and is abominable stuff for yacht use. In a very short time after breaking in, the heart or core breaks in numerous places and works out between the strands to the surface, whereupon it fouls in the blocks and snags on everything. So when buying 4-strand rope be sure it has no core.

Sisal

Sisal fibers are obtained from the leaves of a plant resembling the cactus and is grown principally in Java. Unlike Manila it contains little or no natural oil and therefore has no resistance to moisture. It has but two-thirds the strength of Manila and deteriorates rapidly. Its short, coarse fibers make a rope that is hairy and rough on the hands. Without the protection of natural oils it soaks up water like a sponge and becomes soft and slippery, and in this state it wears out very quickly. Even the best grade of Sisal is inferior to the common grades of Manila, and the yachtsman looks upon it for what it is—a substitute of last resort.

Hemp

The fibers of the Hemp plant formerly occupied the high place in rope making that Manila does today. Before the introduction of wire rope Hemp was universally used for ships' standing rigging, and because it stretches very little it was admirably suited for the purpose. For the same reason sails are roped with Hemp, and the amount of stretch can be gauged and allowed for with remarkable accuracy.

Hemp fibers are short, soft and very fine, with none of the springiness so characteristic of Manila, and this necessitates a different construction. For example, in $\frac{3}{8}$ inch Manila each strand has 4 threads or yarns, while in Hemp rope of the same size each strand is composed of 6 threads laid up about a core or center thread, making 7 in all. It has a harder lay than Manila yet is more ductile. Untreated Hemp rope soaks up water readily and it then becomes so stiff and rigid that it is almost impossible to handle. Therefore it is customarily tarred (impregnated with pine oil), which protects it from water, weather and rot. It has an extremely long life, which makes it very valuable for standing rigging such as lanyards, ratlines and small stuff for seizings, and I shall have more to say about its general usefulness later.

Cotton

Although its use is restricted to what we might call lighter duties, Cotton rope is strictly a yachtsman's rope. Clean, white, pleasing to the eye and smooth to the touch, it has great decorative value and adds much to a yacht's appearance. It is entirely unsuitable for sheets, halyards or heavy work because of its limited strength, poor resistance to chafe, and tendency to become hard, stiff and unmanageable when wet. For light work such as manropes, lashings, pennants and signal lines, or anything of a purely decorative nature it truly *belongs* to a yacht. Because of the soft nature of its fibers it unlays and falls apart when cut, and can be spliced only with difficulty. Containing no natural or added oils it rots easily and has a relatively short life.

Linen

Rope made of linen flax is a high quality product of limited usefulness. For running rigging on sailing craft it has no equal, possessing all of the qualities most desired. It is very soft, limp and flexible, with none of the springy resilience generally expected of rope, and yet it is the strongest natural-fiber rope made. Domestic makes are best, some of the imported ropes having an inclination to stiffen when wet and become long-jawed after breaking in. Log lines and lead lines are generally made of braided linen because of its resistance to shrinking and stretching.

Unfortunately the high cost of Linen rope prevents it from achieving the popularity it rightly deserves, and so it falls into the category of luxury items.

Nylon

Modern science's contribution to rope making, the first practical artificial fiber, has been welcomed by yachtsmen the world over with varying degrees of enthusiasm. In some respects it is superior to all others, but it has certain characteristics restricting its usefulness which should be understood before putting it to work.

Nylon rope is the strongest and most elastic of all. It is impervious to water and rot, can be stowed when wet without deteriorating, seems to last indefinitely and retains its full strength even after hard service. On the other hand it is slick, smooth and slippery to grasp and hold, particularly in the small sizes. It is very difficult to splice, although immersion in boiling water makes the task a little easier. Hold a match flame under it and it will instantly melt, but whether this indicates that long exposure to a hot sun is destructive, I am not prepared to say.

Its almost unbelievable elasticity (almost 29%) makes it just about perfect for anchor cables, mooring lines, sheets and centerboard pennants, but totally unsuitable for halyards. When lying at anchor in heavy seas a Nylon cable acts as a resilient spring, cushioning the shock as the yacht surges to the impact of each wave. This dampening action is pleasurably noticeable to those on board, and the wear and tear on the yacht and its gear is reduced to a minimum.

Nylon sheets have a useful life many times that of Manila. With hard use the outside fibers chafe through much as any other rope, and it gets the slightly fuzzy look that is peculiar to Cotton, but this does not appear to affect its remarkable strength to any marked degree.

Cordage

Under this heading comes what is known as the "small stuff"—all the lines, twines, marline, etc., used for seizings, whippings, lashings and many other applications where something smaller than rope is called for. This list could be quite long, for there is a wide variety of material, but I have chosen only those that are indispensable on the small yacht.

First and foremost is *marline,* the marlinspike sailor's best friend, beloved alike for its myriad of uses and its tarry smell. *Imported Yacht Marline* is the best obtainable. It is made of the finest hemp and lightly tarred, has two strands and is laid up left-handed. Uniformly perfect in construction and very strong, it is invaluable for serving fiber and wire rope, and for the many whippings, seizings and stoppings constantly needed aboard every yacht.

It is put up in half-pound balls in two sizes—"fine," 360 feet per ball, and "medium," 180 feet per ball. Every well-found yacht carries several balls of each. Wet or dry, it is the perfect seizing material, and after months of use it can be removed and re-used with safety. It can be applied by the hands, with a serving mallet or threaded through a sail needle for stitching.

Common domestic marline is greatly inferior, although it too is useful. It is easily recognized by its very dark color and varnished appearance. It is not as strong as the imported kind and costs a third less. When wet it rapidly goes to pieces, and therefore its use should be restricted to temporary jobs.

Braided Cotton Line

This is listed by marine supply firms as "cotton flag halyard," ranging in size from 7/64ths to 5/32nds of an inch in diameter and is sold by the hank of 48 feet. It is handy stuff to have on board—for the numerous light lashings, various lanyards and the making of articles of a decorative nature. It is very strong, easy to handle, and because of its braided construction has very little stretch and does not require whipping.

Seine Twine and Untarred Cod Line

These are very useful for seizings, stoppings and small lashings of a purely temporary nature, to be thrown away after use. Both are of 3-strand cotton, the first soft laid, the second hard laid, and they come in various small sizes. Both unlay very quickly when cut so their period of usefulness is short. In the making of nets and for the decorative arts of the marlinspike you need a lot of this clean white line.

Cotton Rope

Although it has already been discussed under rope materials, small diameter cotton rope also serves as small stuff. It is used for fender lanyards, lashings, grab-lines and pennants, particularly where appearance is important. It cannot be used unless the ends are whipped, for it quickly unlays and frays when cut.

Sail Twine properly belongs under cordage, but it is discussed in detail in the chapter on *Palm-and-Needle Work*.

II

Sailors' Vernacular

The sailor's terminology, while admittedly often picturesque, is usually terse, descriptive and meaningful. In the main, his purpose is to be concise and specific in the giving and receiving of orders, particularly where the necessity of emergencies demands it. However, his expressons are in some instances ambiguous, particularly to the novice. Sailors in the British Navy during World War II were often heard to quote a mythical directive, "The bottom of the box is marked 'TOP' in order to avoid confusion."

In describing and demonstrating the numerous applications of rope and cordage it is imperative that the correct names and expressions be used and clearly understood. So "in order to avoid confusion" I have here compiled a list of those pertinent to the practice of the sailor's arts, with the earnest plea that they be not merely read, but remembered. For the week-end yachtsman to learn and freely use the traditional language of the sea is no affectation, believe me. It contributes to orderly thinking, disciplined action and personal efficiency.

In its generic sense the word *knot* is often applied to all complications in cordage such as turns, tucks and passes, except those of an accidental nature. But the sailor breaks them down into four groups, *knots, hitches, bends* and *splices.* There are two kinds of knots: those used to form a loop, such as the *bowline,* and *knob knots,* with which a knob or bunch is formed in the rope to prevent unreeving, or fraying, or to provide a handhold. Again, there are two kinds of knob knots: the *Stopper Knot,* in which the end of the rope, after forming the knob, passes out of the structure at the top; and the *Button Knot,* in which the end of the rope emerges at the bottom.

A *hitch* is used to make a rope fast to *another object.*

A *bend* secures *two rope ends to each other.*

In constructing any of the above, a rope is considered to have three parts: the *working end,* which is the extremity being manipulated; the *standing part,* which is the inactive part; and the *bight,* which might be described as a curve or arc in the rope no smaller than a semicircle, or any central part of the rope between the ends.

A *lashing* secures one object to another with rope or small stuff.

A *seizing* binds ropes together or to other objects, more or less permanently.

A *stopping* serves much in the same manner, but temporarily.

A *whipping* is a binding of sail-twine or marline placed about a rope-end to prevent its fraying or unlaying.

Worming is the laying-in of small stuff between the strands of a rope to fill up the spaces (known as contlines) and make the rope smoother, and also to prepare the rope for

Parceling, in which a strip of canvas is wound spirally around the rope with the lay, and heavily tarred, after which

A *serving* is applied. Tarred marline is tightly wound about the rope *against the lay.* The act of worming, parceling and serving is referred to as *service,* and is applied to wire and other ropes to keep out moisture. Its use is generally confined to standing rigging. In modern yachts rigged with stainless steel wire of relatively small size, service increases the diameter, decreases chafe, and permits fiber rope or small lines to be hitched to it without slipping. In the case of wire bowsprit shrouds or footropes, service makes them easier on the feet and gives more secure footing.

To *marl* is to secure parceling or canvas chafing gear with a series of *marling hitches,* which are similar to *half-hitches,* but more secure.

As he goes about his duties in these applications of rope and cordage the sailor adheres strictly to his traditional idiomatic language in describing them. He *never* "ties" a knot—for a knot is always *made,* or *put in.* A hitch is *taken* or *made fast.* He *puts in* a splice, *bends* two ropes together, and *works* a Turk's Head knot or a sennit. He *claps on* a seizing or stopping and *clears* a tangled rope by *overhauling* it. Rope is always coiled *down,* never up, and if the coil must be turned over he will *capsize* it. He will *secure for sea* by lashing everything movable above decks and *freshen the nip* of a sheet, halyard or cable by taking up or slackening a bit, to bring the wear or chafe in a different place.

III

Some Sailor's Tools and Their Use

The arts of the marlinspike are fundamentally simple, and since their applications are somewhat limited aboard the average small yacht you do not need an elaborate array of tools and equipment. Indeed, the professional sailor for countless centuries has practiced many of his skills with the aid of nothing more than his knife, his marlinspike and his hands. The manual dexterity acquired through long years of working with rope and cordage was undoubtedly responsible for the old saying which so aptly describes him: "—every finger a marlinspike, his blood of Stockholm tar."

The sailor's one indispensable tool was his knife, as much a mark of his calling as the tattooed maiden on his hairy chest. Sharp, sheathed and belted just above his starboard buttock, it was ready at hand for working, eating or fighting. Invariably he had made it himself, starting with an old file painstakingly ground to the peculiar shape he considered important, and finishing with a sheath decorated or embellished to suit his fancy, and into the making went many a watch below.

Admitting that the situations facing the professional

seaman of old differ greatly from those with which we are concerned, a proper seagoing knife is equally indispensable to the yachtsman, even though he may not engage in knife brawls and follows Emily Post in the choice of eating tools. Nor is it necessary that he laboriously make his own, for there are a number of excellent knives on the market which have been designed by yachtsmen for yachtsmen. It is important, however, to know what constitutes a proper knife before attempting to make a choice, and so I suggest we consider the features most desired and the manner in which it will be used.

Of course it will be used most often in the cutting of rope and cordage, and occasionally canvas. In emergencies it will double for a hatchet and split wood for the galley fire, clean a mess of fish or open clams. Its work will be on the heavy side and it must be rugged enough to withstand hard use without fear of failure.

The shape of the blade is of the utmost importance. The tip or point should be blunt—the closer it approaches the shape of a meat cleaver the better. The sharp point of the hunting or skinning knife is unsuitable and dangerous. The cutting edge should be straight or but slightly curved throughout its length, without the sudden round at the tip found in most penknives. The blade should be short, 4 to 4½ inches at most, and quite wide, from 1 to 1¼ inches. It should be thick, in section a true wedge-shape, and carry its thickness right out to the back.

The handle should be hefty and well-shaped to give the user a firm grip without tiring the hand, and wide enough to prevent the knife from turning in the hand.

Of course the end of the handle should have a hole or a shackle to take a lanyard.

There are two types of knives available—the rigid, one-piece sheath knife, worn at the belt, and the folding clasp knife generally carried in the pocket. The clasp knife appears to outsell the sheath knife by at least two

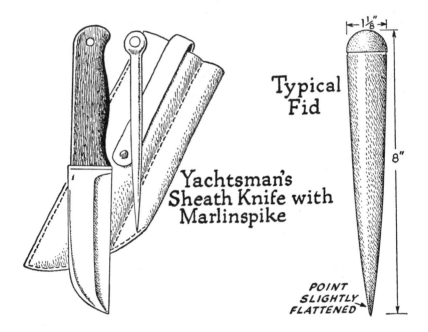

Typical
Fid

1⅛"

8"

Yachtsman's
Sheath Knife with
Marlinspike

POINT
SLIGHTLY
FLATTENED

to one, but this does not necessarily imply superiority—advertising and distribution may be the reason, plus the fact that there are more companies making them.

The clasp knives are generally pretty much alike in their basic construction. The majority have a 4-inch blade and a small marlinspike which folds into the back. Some have a device by which the blade is locked in the open position, a very desirable feature. When using the knife the marlinspike on the back makes the handle rather uncomfortable and tiring. Its principle virtue is its compactness, and since the average man normally carries his knife in his pocket this may account for its popularity.

The sheath knife, on the other hand, is too large and of the wrong shape to fit in one's pocket and can be carried in but one place, at the belt. It is worn over the right hip near the center of the back, and at first feels rather awkward, but, like the wearing of false teeth, you soon get used to it. Because the blade and its tang are of one piece, a sheath knife is much stronger than the clasp knife, cannot collapse or fold up in use, and has no springs to break. In choosing a knife of this type be sure that the sheath or scabbard encloses the entire knife, blade and handle, with just the *end* of the handle exposed. Otherwise the handle will snag on everything and the knife will slip out.

Years of experience with both types have convinced me that the sheath knife is superior to the clasp knife on several counts. First and foremost, it takes two hands to open a clasp knife, and wet fingers with limp fingernails are not always dependable. In an emergency, using one hand to hold on with, it is quite a feat to open the knife with the free hand without dropping it. Then too, it must first be fished out of the pocket, and all too often a handkerchief, sail stop, or a tangled wad of marline has been crammed in on top of the knife.

But the sheath knife is always instantly accessible. One quick, backhanded swipe and the hand comes up with the knife ready for action. I'll admit that for the normal, leisurely use about the deck one type is as efficient as the other, but in the critical emergency, where speed and sureness are vital, the sheath knife is superior.

The reason for devoting so much space to such a simple matter as choosing a knife is directly traceable to a very unpleasant experience I had several years ago. In the evening of an oppressive day in July my wife and I sought relief from the heat by a sail in our 33-foot auxiliary ketch. After a long beat to windward in a light northeasterly I came about and headed for home, the booms broad off and running dead before it.

Suddenly, with hardly five seconds' warning, we were struck by the most vicious line squall I have ever encountered in more than thirty years of yachting. We were caught in the worst possible position—dead before the wind and in total darkness. In an instant the boat rounded to and broached. She lay at a critical angle of heel with the boom-ends in the water, the sails flogging wildly and every sheet, halyard and line hopelessly fouled or washed overboard. For an instant I was too dazed and shocked by the suddenness of it all to do anything but hang on.

I waited several moments to see if the boat would right herself, but she seemed to be pressing down even further and I knew that the canvas had to come off in a hurry. I clawed my way forward, yanked out my sheath knife and cut the main and jib halyards just above the belaying pins. After what seemed like an hour I got the sails nearly all of the way down, and slowly the boat righted to a less critical angle of heel.

Hours later, in the peaceful security of my sheltered mooring I gave silent thanks for the friend who but recently had given me that sheath knife, for without it I doubt if I could have got the sails off in time to prevent capsizing. I learned many things that night, not the least of which was the importance of a proper knife.

In splicing or other work requiring the opening of the strands of rope one's fingers are often inadequate, and a marlinspike or fid must be employed. There are two kinds of spikes—one used for wire rope, which has a "head," or knob at the end, and the other for fiber rope, which has no head and is just a straight, tapered cone from point to handle. Made of tool steel and highly polished, they average about eight inches in length. A seizing can be pulled up considerably tighter with a marlinspike than with the hands alone by using it as a lever, merely taking a hitch about the point with the marline.

Aboard the average small yacht most of the work is done with rope of relatively small diameter, rarely over an inch, and many men dispense with the marlinspike and work with the fingers alone. However, some individuals are "all thumbs" and have a trying time, even with the aid of a spike. It depends on the individual, but it has been my experience that the learner has far less trouble if he uses the spike. In turning in a splice, as an instance, the tool having been entered into the rope preparatory to tucking a strand can be *left in position* while the worker lights his pipe and ponders the next move. However, whether you use the fingers, marlinspike or fid, it is the result that counts, not the method.

A fid serves much the same purpose as the marlinspike but is made of wood. Those carried by marine supply houses are generally made of hickory or ash, but lignum vitae is superior, being a denser and therefore heavier wood. Every yachtsman should have a fid in his ditty bag, and anyone having a lathe can turn one out easily, so for those who would make their own the accompanying illustration gives the typical shape and dimensions suitable for the small yacht.

While the small marlinspike, such as those fitted to clasp knives, are very versatile and useful tools and handy for opening screw shackles and withdrawing cotter pins, a fid is preferable for splicing fiber rope. When entering between the strands the sharp spike invariably pierces or picks up some fibers from one or the other, and a foul splice results; but the blunter point of the fid slips through cleanly, and is much kinder to the rope.

Generally speaking, the fid is much thicker in proportion to its length and thus has a quicker or shorter taper, so you gain a larger opening in the rope for ease in tucking the strands. This you will find a most desirable feature when working with rope of large diameter, such as an anchor cable.

Fids are also useful tools of the sailmaker, for "sticking" cringles and sail thimbles, and various other jobs, and I shall discuss these applications in the chapter on canvas work. There are also other sailor's tools for special work which are necessary to the yachtsman, which will be taken up in detail in the chapter devoted to the sailor's ditty bag.

While on the subject of tools it would be pertinent to consider a minor, though useful detail in the handling of rope, and that is the method of cutting it. I have noticed that the amateur will invariably grasp a bight of the rope, hook his knife blade under it and yank or pull it sharply toward him. It never cuts entirely through on the first try, so he finishes by sawing back and forth on the uncut fibers and the severed ends then look ragged and ratty. Besides being a dangerous practice it is distinctly unseamanlike. After whippings have been applied the rope should be cut square and clean. Place the rope on the deck, rail or any smooth, hard surface and lay the blade of the sheath knife across it squarely. Then tap or strike the back of the knife with a fid, marlinspike or even the heel of your hand until all but a few of the fibers are cut. With a little practice you can cut rope in this manner even on a varnished surface without marring it.

IV

Basic Knots

The Reef Knot

The Reef Knot, often called the Square Knot, is probably the most universally known and remembered of all knots. From the sailor's viewpoint this is extremely unfortunate, for many lives have been needlessly lost through its indiscriminate use by the uninitiated. At sea it is customarily employed in lashings and seizings, and in reefing or furling sails, and for these alone it is excellent. But *under no circumstances should it ever be used as a bend,* to tie two ropes together. If the two ends are of unequal size, or one rope is stiffer or smoother than the other the knot is almost certain to spill and slip.

If you grasp one of the free ends and jerk it across the knot it will instantly capsize into a pair of reversed half-hitches which can be stripped off with one hand. It is this characteristic, the ease with which it can be spilled, which makes it so valuable as a reefing knot.

All knots, bends and hitches tend to tighten up and are more difficult to untie when they become wet, and the Reef Knot is a notable offender in this respect.

Therefore it is always modified to a *Slipped Reef Knot* when used for reefing and lashings, where speed and sureness are vitally important.

Sail battens are tied in the batten pockets with the Reef Knot, and on occasion the shaking of the sail will spill the knot, resulting in the loss of the batten. I have found that this can be avoided by tying an extra half-knot on top of the Reef Knot.

The Bowline

For hundreds of years the Bowline has been the most useful of all sailor's knots. Used to tie a loop in a rope end, it has all of the attributes of an ideal knot: it is easily and quickly tied, has great strength with no tendency to slip, and can be readily untied even when wet or after being subjected to great strain.

Notice in the illustration that the working end of the rope lies on the *inside* of the loop. This is known as a Right-handed Bowline, and many beginners unwittingly tie the knot with the end on the outside of the loop, which makes it a Left-handed Bowline, a much inferior form.

On occasion a loop is desired in the middle of a rope, where the rope has been doubled for added strength, and this calls for the *Bowline in the Bight*. It consists of two loops instead of one, and is particularly useful for slinging a tackle, because wherever possible a hook should have a double bearing when hitched to a rope. For this reason care should be taken in drawing up the knot so that the two loops are of equal length.

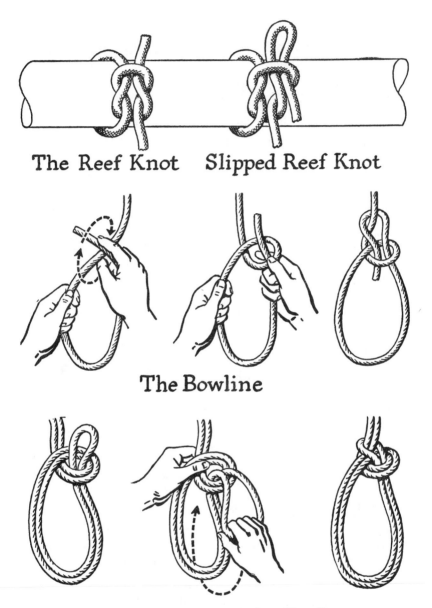

The Reef Knot   Slipped Reef Knot

The Bowline

The Bowline on the Bight

The Figure-Eight Knot

Because sheets will sometimes get away from you and start to run out through the blocks some sort of *stopper* knot should be tied in the bitter ends to prevent them from completely unreeving. In light airs it is often but

The Figure Eight Knot

The Constrictor Knot...doubled...slipped

a minor annoyance to lose a sheet, but when a mainsheet "goes by the run" in heavy weather it can have tragic consequences. Hence the importance of such a small detail as a stopper knot.

There are many such knots, some rather complicated, but the Figure-Eight is most commonly used. It can be tied quickly and easily, forms a knot large enough to prevent its passing through a block, and is easy to untie. It should be noted in passing that this or any other stopper knot does *not* take the place of a whipping when tied in a rope end, as many novices assume. *Every* rope end should be whipped regardless of how or where it is used.

The Constrictor Knot

This knot was invented or contrived by the late Clifford Ashley, the foremost authority on knots, to take the place of the common seizing or stopping. It is nothing more than a half-knot with a round turn over it, and should be tied only in "small stuff," never in rope.

In many respects the Constrictor Knot is superior to a common seizing. It is quicker, neater, and can be drawn up much more tightly. The harder you pull the two ends the tighter it grips, and it *will not slacken when you let go* . . . you can hold all you gain. It can be set up so tightly that it is almost impossible to untie it, and for that reason it makes an excellent whipping. For a *permanent* whipping, however, an extra round turn should be taken, as shown in the illustration.

For a temporary seizing or stopping it can be tied as a *slipped knot,* as illustrated, which makes it easier to untie. Just tuck a bight instead of the single working end.

The Constrictor Knot is not very well known, but its superior construction and usefulness leads me to believe that it ultimately will achieve the popularity it rightly deserves.

V

Useful Hitches and Bends

There are over a hundred different hitches which may be used to make a rope fast to various objects, each designed for a specific application. Of these there are six which I feel every yachtsman should know. Hitches are employed in making fast to such things as a pile, bitt, spar, rail, ring or hook, and it should be obvious that no one hitch will suffice for all. These six will adequately cover the needs of the average small yacht, for in choosing them I have given careful consideration to every phase of operation and maintenance in which a hitch would be employed.

The Clove Hitch

This is the most commonly used of all hitches. It is the quickest to tie and the easiest to remember. It can be tied with one hand or two, and as easily by night as by day. It consists of two Single Hitches, the second superimposed on the first, and is used for securing to any cylindrical object such as a post, bollard, spar or rail where the pull will be exerted *at an angle*. It is commonly used in dock lines as a temporary mooring, to se-

31

cure fender lines to a rail, various lashings, and serves as a *crossing knot* when rigging ratlines or lifelines, to name but a few.

The *Clove Hitch* must never be considered as really *secure,* and had best be regarded as a general utility hitch for temporary use. It cannot be drawn up snugly by pulling on one end only, and there is always an unpredictable amount of initial slip when a strain is put on it. It will loosen and slip if subjected to intermittent pulls in different directions, or if placed over a *square* post or piling.

There are two important points to remember when using the *Clove Hitch*—always set it up snugly by hand before putting a strain on it, and never use it where great strength and safety are required, for it is not a heavy-duty hitch. It is good practice to add a single hitch around the standing part of the line with the working end, when tying up to a dock.

The Rolling Hitch

This is the hitch to use in securing a rope to a spar for *a lengthwise pull.* Its chief virtue is its ability to hold without slipping when tied on a very smooth surface. In stepping and unshipping a mast it secures the sling to which the tackle is hooked. When aloft in a boatswain's chair a life line should always be made fast to the mast with a *Rolling Hitch,* for it will not slip even if your weight should suddenly fall on it. In securing a light line to wire standing rigging, which is extremely slick and slippery, this is the hitch to use.

You will note in the illustration that not less than two

The Clove Hitch

The Rolling Hitch

The Fisherman's Bend

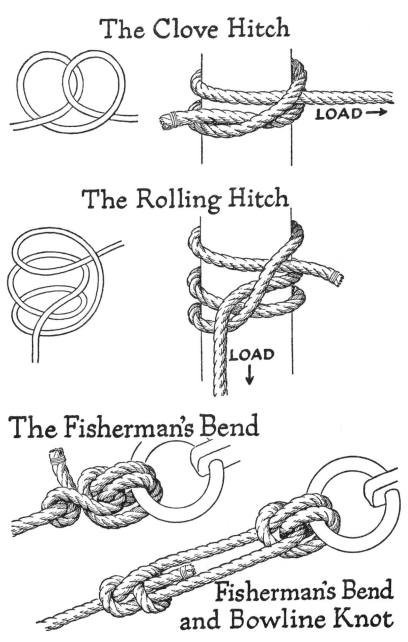

LOAD →

LOAD ↓

Fisherman's Bend and Bowline Knot

round turns are taken about the spar below the standing part counter-clockwise, and the working end is brought up over all and finished off with one or two single hitches about the spar to the right. *Always* set the hitch up snugly and carefully before putting a strain on it. One of the best features of the *Rolling Hitch* is that it may be slid up or down with one hand to any point on the spar and still will set up securely the instant it is subjected to a load.

The Fisherman's Bend

The sailor always *bends* a rope to an anchor, which accounts for this hitch being termed a *bend*. Often called the *Anchor Bend,* it is one of the strongest of all hitches. It consists of a round turn with a hitch through the turns and two single hitches about the standing part. An anchor ring is always considerably smaller in diameter than the warp or cable, and the bearing surface is therefore so small that there is severe chafe and distortion of the rope. The *Fisherman's Bend* having *two* parts of the rope passing through the ring, gives the maximum bearing surface possible and reduces the amount of wear and chafe at this point.

It should be noted here that not all anchors are equipped with a ring. Some of the modern patent anchors have a shackle at the end of the shank instead of a ring. I have found that the shackle is generally too small to admit more than one turn of the cable, and the *Fisherman's Bend* cannot be used. This can be corrected by adding a larger shackle of not less than 3 inch diameter.

While the hitch itself is amply strong and secure, the

chafe and wear of the ring will in time weaken the rope. It is therefore advisable to frequently inspect the rope at the ring for signs of wear and occasionally shift the hitch a few inches to bring the ring to a different part of the rope.

It is conceivable that hard use and a rocky bottom could in time loosen or dislodge the hitches on the standing part, and this could mean the loss of the anchor. To insure against this danger I suggest the use of the *Fisherman's Bend* and *Bowline Knot,* which is infinitely more secure and just as easy to tie. As shown in the illustration, the single hitches are eliminated and a *Bowline Knot* is tied in their stead.

The Marlinspike Hitch

This hitch is so simple that instructions for tying it are unnecessary. In splicing, seizing and serving the hands alone are not strong enough to draw up the turns of marline as tightly as desired. With this hitch tied about the marlinspike a powerful purchase can be had, and the spike can be used as a lever, with the rope as a fulcrum. Seizings are of no value unless they are extremely tight, and the *Marlinspike Hitch* is a very practical aid in achieving a perfect job.

The Double Becket Hitch

It is often necessary to secure a line to an eye splice or loop, and a hitch is needed which can be tied quickly and as readily untied. The *Becket Hitch* is the most practical hitch for the purpose, and is secure and dependable. The working end is brought up through the

The Marlinspike Hitch

The Double Becket Hitch

FALL

The Boatswain's Hitch

loop and passed around the loop twice, each time going under the standing part. Although it may look somewhat insecure it sets up very tightly under a strain. It was used by whalers to bend the whaleline to the becket of the harpoon, which is indicative of its great strength and the reliance put upon it. Another use for this hitch is in bending a rope to the hook of a tackle block, care being taken to see that the rope is of sufficient diameter to fill the hook snugly.

The Boatswain's Hitch

Although it is used but infrequently, this hitch is invaluable when going aloft in a boatswain's chair. When varnishing a mast it is necessary to change position many times, lowering away and stopping as required. The simplest means of securing the fall of the tackle is to use this hitch as shown in the illustration. Holding the fall with one hand, the other hand pulls a bight forward under the eye seizing and a half turn of the wrist forms a single hitch, which is then placed over the bill of the hook of the tackle block. By this means you eliminate the need for a helper on deck, and can take comfort in knowing that your life is in your own hands.

A *bend* is used to unite two rope ends, to lengthen a rope that does not pass through a block. It is most commonly used in making up a towline or in lengthening an anchor cable. It must possess maximum strength without slipping and must be easy to untie even when soaking wet. The three bends shown here have these characteristics and are entirely reliable.

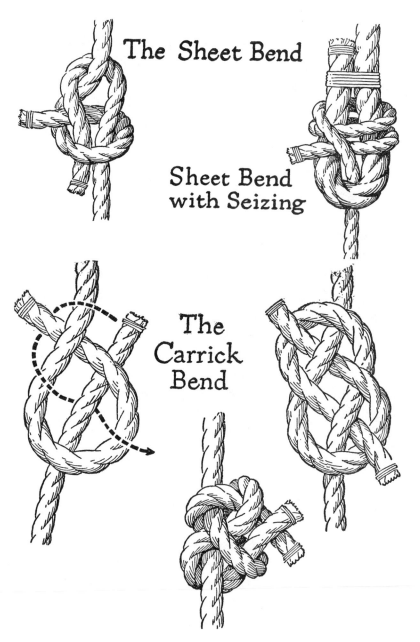

The Sheet Bend

Sheet Bend with Seizing

The Carrick Bend

The Sheet Bend

This is a general utility bend. It will serve for almost every purpose, can be tied in an instant and can always be untied no matter how wet and tight it may be. It is tied in the same manner as the *Bowline Knot,* but instead of tying an end to its own bight, it is tied to a bight in another end. Caution—always draw it up snugly *by hand* before putting a strain on it.

I have also shown the *Double Sheet Bend with Seizing,* which is a variation having greater security and should be used in preference where one rope is larger than the other. An eye is seized in the larger rope and the smaller end is rove through as shown. You will note that it is similar to the *Double Becket Hitch,* except that the latter is tied in a *spliced* eye or loop.

The Carrick Bend

This is the nearest thing to a perfect bend. There is no other so strong or secure, and it can be untied quickly and easily. It is a heavy-duty bend, highly recommended for towing lines and moorings. I have observed that many yachtsmen fail to use this bend because they have difficulty in remembering how it is tied, but because of its superior qualities and its unquestioned value I believe it warrants a little extra time being spent in learning the manner in which it is put together. The best way to learn, or I should say to *remember* this or any other knot, hitch or bend, is to tie it many times, at *intervals of several days,* until the sequence of its movements are firmly fixed in your mind.

VI

The Art of Splicing

In Chapter I, I emphasized the importance of understanding the structural characteristics of rope, the nature of its parts and the manner in which it is put together. I know of no better way to learn its peculiarities and get the feel of working with it than in splicing. Of all the ancient arts of the sailor there is none more useful or important, and to put in a first-class splice you must have a fundamental understanding of rope's basic construction.

Splicing, like matrimony, should not be undertaken lightly, nor can it be done hurriedly. It requires patient, careful study to attain proficiency, and even then speed is neither necessary nor desirable. It is the sort of work one does when there is plenty of time, ashore or lying at moorings.

There are four useful splices every yachtsman should know: the *Eye Splice*, the *Short Splice*, the *Long Splice* and the *Grommet*. It may seem odd to include the *Grommet* but it is actually a form of *Long Splice*, in which but a single rope strand is used.

Eye Splices are needed almost continually, *Short*

40

Splices only infrequently, and *Long Splices* much less. *Grommets* are very useful in working with canvas, making rope-stropped blocks and various articles of ship's gear.

Although the *methods* used in splicing are pretty

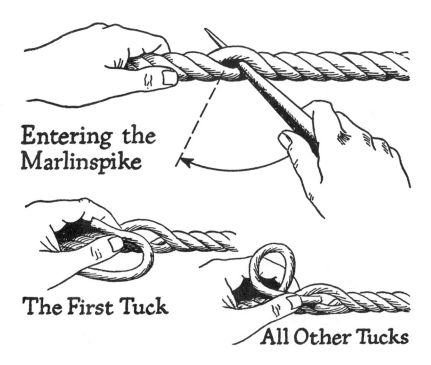

Entering the Marlinspike

The First Tuck

All Other Tucks

much alike the world over, the *techniques* employed vary with the individual. There are some, including myself, who will not use a marlinspike or fid unless forced to. There are others who can't put a splice in ¼ inch line unless they have a large kit of assorted tools at hand. From where I sit, if you can put in a professional splice neatly and efficiently it is of small matter whether you use your fingers, fid or bobby-pins—it's the end result that's important.

For the beginner, however, a marlinspike or fid is very necessary. It enables you to lift a strand and keep it opened while you study the next tuck, and with less distortion of the lay of the rope than might occur with untrained fingers.

The first illustration shows the correct way to enter the marlinspike into the rope. Notice that it goes under the strand *with the lay* and then is rotated clockwise a quarter of a turn to open up the rope. Extreme care must be taken when entering the spike to be certain that you do not pick up any fibers from the adjacent strands —it should go exactly between the strands.

The second illustration shows how to make the *first* tuck with any given strand. Turn the end of the strand back *counterclockwise* and push it through the opening.

The third illustration shows how to make *all succeeding* tucks. A left twist is given the strand, forming a left turn, and note that the end points to the *right* instead of to the left as in the preceding illustration.

The reason for the different methods of tucking is that the first tuck should be made without disturbing the lay of the strand, while the second method *removes* some of the twist from the working strand so that it will lay fairly over the next strand.

I earnestly recommend that you obtain six or eight feet of tarred hemp rope to practice splicing with. If your yacht supply house does not stock it you can get it from any sailmaker. It is beautiful stuff to work with, can be used over and over and still be restored to its original lay.

The Eye Splice

Let us assume you have a length of 3/8 inch rope, which is the size I recommend for practice. About six or eight inches from the end put on a tight seizing of sail twine or marline, using the *Constrictor Knot* (Page 29). Now unlay the rope to the seizing and put a similar seizing or whipping on the end of each strand. Remember that you must preserve the natural lay of the strands at all times.

Referring to Diagram 1, bring the working end up to the right to form a loop or eye. Now grasp the standing part firmly and untwist the rope at the point where you wish to start the splice. Here is where the beginner invariably goes haywire—right at the start where the first tucks are made, so let's stop right here and study the diagram until the sequence of tucks is firmly fixed in your mind.

Reading from left to right, you will notice that I have labeled the working strands A, B, and C, and the strands of the standing part, under which they are to be tucked, *a, b,* and *c.* I have done this merely to co-ordinate the diagrams with these instructions, but the strands of the rope in your hands are not numbered or labeled, and when putting in a splice you would look rather silly trying to remember which strand is A and which is *c.* Therefore you should always think of the three strands as the left-hand, the center, and the right-hand strands.

All tucks are made *against the lay,* from the right to

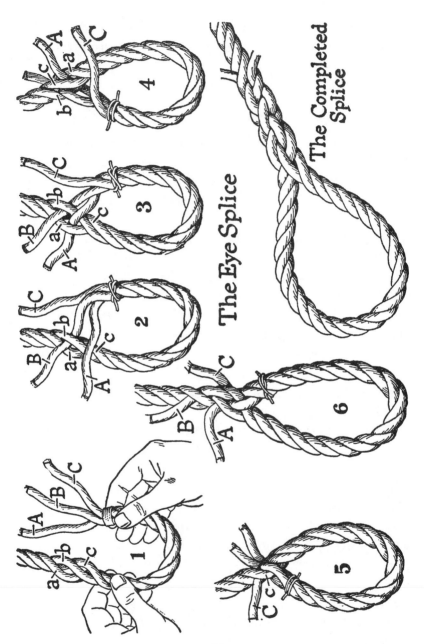

The Eye Splice

The Completed Splice

44

the left. Now again referring to Diagram 1, left-hand strand A of the working end is tucked under *a* of the standing part, center strand B is tucked under *b,* and the right-hand strand C is tucked under the right-hand strand *c.* Fix that sequence firmly in your mind—left under left, center under center and right under right.

Always tuck the *center strand first,* the left-hand next and the right-hand *last.* Diagram 2 shows the first tuck, center strand B tucked under center strand *b* to the left side.

Diagram 3 shows the second tuck, with strand A going over *b* and under *a.* Now in order to tuck the last strand, C, it is necessary to flop the whole works over to get at it from the back. Diagram 4 shows how it will appear in this position. Notice that strand C is now on the left side and strand *c* is in a more accessible position.

In Diagram 5 strand C has been tucked under *c,* *from the right.* All three strands having now been tucked once, they should be drawn up snugly, with the seizing lying as close up to the standing part as it comfortably can. See that each strand lies fairly and emerges from the rope opposite the other two.

You are now ready to start the second round of tucks, each strand in turn being passed *over* the strand next to it on the left and then tucked *under* the next or second strand to the left. It makes no difference which strand you start with—in Diagram 6 it happens to be strand B, with which the splice was originally started. Notice that it passes over *a* and is tucked under the next strand to the left.

Continue by tucking the other two strands over one

and under one to the left. All three strands have now been tucked twice. Tuck each strand once more, in turn, and the splice is completed.

Now that we have completed the sequence of tucks, let us look into some of the finer points which determine whether the splice is good or bad. First and foremost it is absolutely imperative that each of the tucked strands be drawn up with equal tension, no one being looser than the others, or the splice will be weak. Each strand should bear an equal share of the load. Furthermore, in drawing up a strand after tucking do *not* pull it back toward the eye or loop, but rather in a direction nearly parallel with the standing part. This is a common mistake with beginners, and only results in a lumpy splice with the strands unnaturally distorted.

Before starting your first tucks hold the working end at the seizing and *untwist the rope a half a turn*, otherwise you'll get a twisted loop which will never stay open. After completing all the tucks, and *before* cutting off the strand ends, lay the splice down on the deck and roll it back and forth under your foot. This tends to fair up the strands and correct any unequal tension you may have got in them.

Under no circumstance should you cut the strands off close to the rope. When a splice is put to work and strain is put on it the strands gradually work back into the rope, so a safe rule in cutting them off is to have the length of the ends equal the diameter of the rope—with $\frac{1}{2}$ inch rope the ends should be left at least half an inch long.

Splicing an eye in 4-strand rope involves the same procedure that is employed with 3-strand, but the *start* is different. You will notice in the accompanying illustration that the first, or left-hand strand is tucked under *two* strands. The second strand is tucked under one, and the remaining two are tucked as in the 3-strand splice, by turning the splice over.

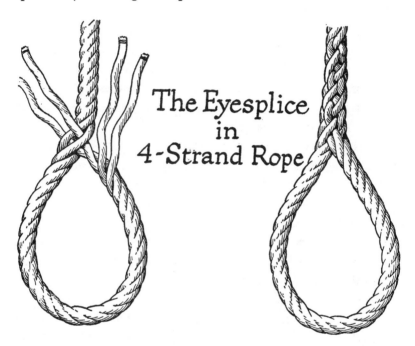

The Eyesplice
in
4-Strand Rope

After the first set of tucks have been made you may continue by tucking the remainder over one and under one as previously described. If you will examine the illustration of the finished splice, however, you may detect a different method. I have made the second and third round of tucks *over one and under two*. In my estimation this makes for a stronger and neater splice when working with 4-strand rope, and the strands lie more fairly.

Should the 4-strand rope you are working with have a heart or core it must be cut out in the "crotch" of the unlayed strands just short of the first tuck.

The Short Splice

Whenever it is necessary to bend two ropes together permanently the *Short Splice* is used, except, of course, where the rope must render through a block. It doubles the diameter of the rope at the splice and therefore is impractical for running rigging, for which the *Long Splice* is used exclusively.

In the *Short Splice* all tucks are made over one and under one against the lay, from right to left, just as you did with the *Eye Splice*. Here, too, it is vitally important that every strand be tucked alike, with equal tension in every part. Just one slack strand can cause the splice to fail under stress. A splice can't be hurried—every strand must be carefully worked into position and adjusted for fairness after every tuck.

You start as usual, putting a temporary whipping on every strand. Put a seizing on each rope about six inches from the end and unlay each rope to the seizing. I am assuming you are practicing with ⅜ or ½ inch rope—the larger the rope the farther it must be unlaid.

Now clutch the two ropes together as in Diagram 1. You will note that each strand of one rope lies between two strands of the other rope. Bring them up close together and clap on a narrow, tight seizing where they join, as in Diagram 2. As I stated before, the Constrictor

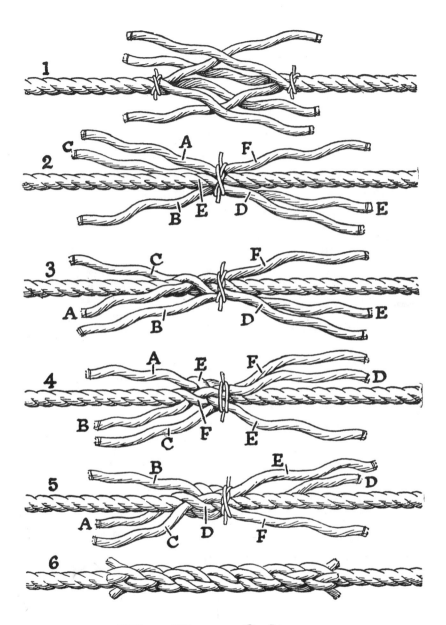

The Short Splice

Knot makes an excellent seizing in splicing. The first two seizings can now be removed and you are ready to tuck the strands.

The first tuck is made as in Diagram 3, with strand A laid over strand D and tucked under strand E.

To make the second tuck rotate the splice away from you and lay strand B over E and tuck it under F, as in Diagram 4.

Rotate the splice away from you another third of a turn and tuck strand C over F and under D as in Diagram 5. This completes the first set of tucks in the left-hand half of the splice. Continue by tucking the three strands a second and then a third time in a like manner.

Now turn the rope and the half-completed splice around on your lap, thus bringing strands D, E and F on the left side. Make three rounds of tucks with these strands exactly as you did with strands A, B, and C, and the splice is completed. Cut off the strand ends, first rolling the splice back and forth under your foot to fair up the strands, and remove the seizing at the center. The finished splice should now look like Diagram 6.

Although the splice is amply strong and secure when made as described, its appearance is a little crude. The rather abrupt "shoulders" of the splice, with the strand ends protruding are continually fetching up against various obstructions and in time the splice takes on a bedraggled, frowsy look. This can be avoided by making a *tapered* splice, which is much handsomer and gives better service.

A *tapered splice* is made by cutting out some of the yarns in each strand, thus progressively reducing its diameter towards the end. The first tuck is always made with the full strand—some splicers make *two* full tucks before tapering. After the first or second tuck, lift up the strand and cut out a third of the yarns, on the *under side* so the cut ends will be hidden. Now tuck the reduced strand and again lift it up and cut out half of the yarns underneath. Tuck once more and trim off the end. Thus you have made four tucks—twice full, once two-thirds and once one-third.

Eye Splices should also be tapered. I make a practice of tapering every splice, not only for appearance but to prevent the strand ends from coming loose. I make six tucks, cutting out but a little from each strand, and by the time the end is reached the strand is so small it is difficult to determine where the splice really starts.

The Long Splice

Occasionally a sheet or halyard is damaged at one point from unobserved chafe or misuse. If the rope is in otherwise good condition it would be foolish to discard it when it is so easy to repair it with a *Long Splice.* While it shortens the rope about three feet, I have found it seldom that running rigging is cut so close to the minimum requirement that it will not permit the splice if needed.

Cut out the damaged part and put a temporary whipping on each strand. Now very carefully unlay the strands of both ropes for a distance of about 15 or 18 inches and clutch them together just as you did for the *Short Splice,* and as I have shown in Diagram 1.

Take the two opposing *center strands,* B and E, and

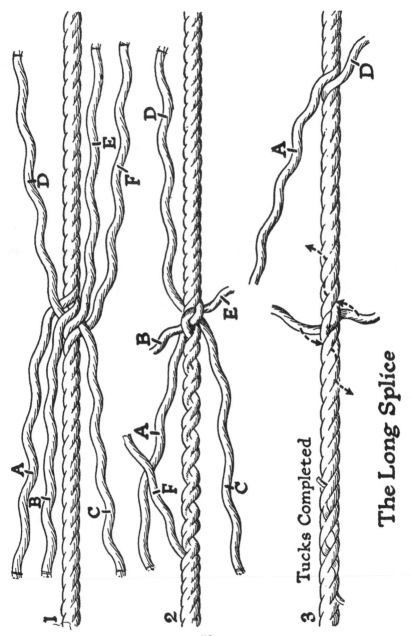

The Long Splice

1

2 Tucks Completed

3

tie a *left-hand half-knot,* as shown in Diagram 2. Do not cut the strands off, and do not draw the half-knot up tightly. In the illustration I have lopped off the strands for the sake of clarity.

Next unlay strand F, and, as you do so, lay in strand C, following as closely to F as possible. When you reach a point about 12 inches to the left, tie a half-knot, just as you did with strands B and E, and tuck the strands as shown in Diagram 3.

In like manner unlay strand A 12 inches to the right, laying strand D in its place and half-knotting them together. You now have a single span of rope, with three half-knots 12 inches apart. Here is the critical point where the beginner often goes wrong. You must go over every inch of the splice and examine every strand for tightness or looseness. Each strand must have the same lay and tension throughout or the splice will be worthless.

If you find one strand that is looser than the rest it must be unlaid and repositioned. The half-knots should be drawn up snugly without undue tension. I neglected to mention that in tying the knots the strands should be *untwisted* a half a turn to flatten them a bit and make the knots less bulky. Each strand is tucked once, then half of the yarns are cut out underneath and the remaining half are tucked once more. Now roll the splice under your foot to flatten the knots, cut off the strands and the job is done.

Don't expect the splice to be invisible, although it is possible with a more elaborate technique. It is enough that it be uniformly smooth and even, and with a mod-

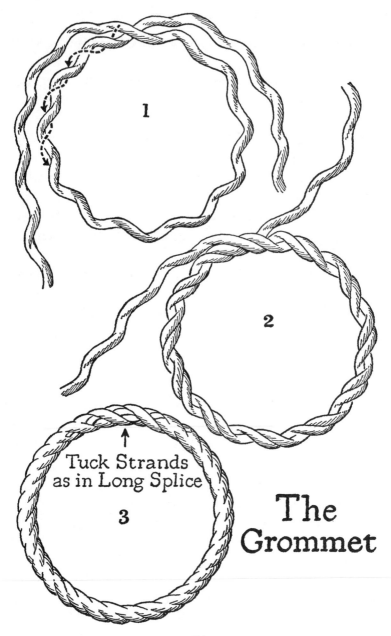

1

2

Tuck Strands
as in Long Splice

3

The Grommet

erate degree of success it will fly through the blocks with the greatest of ease.

The Grommet

The yachtsman will find that many projects call for the making of grommets, ranging from tiny half-inch ones made of tarred marline for eyelet holes in canvaswork, up to large ones of rope for making deck buckets. Three inch cotton grommets make excellent drawer pulls, and rope-stropped blocks require grommets of tarred hemp.

Grommets are nothing more than a single rope strand laid up about itself to form a ring of three strands. The length of the strand required must be three times the circumference of the grommet, plus seven times the circumference of the rope. Thus, a ½ inch rope grommet 7 inches in diameter will require a strand not less than 24½ inches long. It's best to allow a little extra and be on the safe side.

From a length of new rope unlay a strand very carefully to the length required, cut it off and put a temporary whipping on each end. Form a ring with it to the desired diameter by laying the right hand part across and *in front of* the left part, as shown in the first illustration. Now lay up the strand about itself twice, and if one end is expended lay in the other in the opposite direction. Make sure the strands are evenly laid, and when the two ends meet tie a left-hand half-knot and tuck them just as you do in the *Long Splice*.

Grommets made of soft cotton rope require more skill. When a strand is taken from the rope it immediately loses its lay. Thus, when making a grommet it is necessary to impart constantly a *left twist* to the strand as you lay it up to the *right*.

Grommets of marline are made just as rope ones are, but the ends are merely half-knotted without tucking. No matter what kind of grommets you are making the lay of the strand *must* be preserved at all times, for when it is finished it should present the appearance of three strand rope that has never been unlaid.

VII

Whippings

One of the most important "little" jobs on shipboard is the whipping of all rope ends to prevent them from unlaying and to make them easy to reeve through blocks and eyes. Yet because they are a small detail, or perhaps due to an impatient desire to get under way, all too often they are slighted for something which seems at the moment far more important. There is nothing more unseamanlike than a gouty, cow-tailed rope end, and a good whipping is a detail that deserves more care than it often gets.

If you have an observant eye you will see some mighty terrible whippings on very fine yachts, and it is not necessarily indicative of any personal characteristics of the owners, for it happens in the best of families—a haphazard winding of grocery string or any odd piece of twine that happened to be handy, and held in place by a knot and a prayer. Or what is worse, the rope end tied in a half-knot and no whipping at all. There are times, it would seem, when it is a question of which needs the whipping more, the rope or the sailor.

Whippings are put on with either sail twine or marline, depending on the size of the rope. Although there is no hard and fast rule, I use marline on all rope over ¾ inches in diameter. When sail twine is used it should be well waxed with sailmaker's beeswax, to make it lay better and to provide a measure of waterproofing.

Beginners generally try to put the whipping on the very end of the rope, which is incorrect. It should be put on several inches from the end, and when completed the excess rope should be neatly cut off *not less than ⅜ths of an inch* from the whipping. The turns are taken *against* the lay of the rope, working *towards* the end. The *width* of the whipping should equal the diameter of the rope, except where the whipping is purely decorative, in which case it may be several inches long.

The Common Whipping

This is the simplest type of whipping and the one most commonly seen. The twine is laid along the rope to the right in a loop, and the required number of turns are taken over it, as tightly as possible. Then the working end is passed through the loop and hauled back out of sight under the turns by pulling on the left-hand end, and both ends are then trimmed off short.

From my experience I would consider this whipping suitable only for *temporary* use. Time and again I have seen this type come loose, particularly on reef points, where the constant flogging of the rope end caused the ends of the whipping to work down into the contline, the space between the strands of the rope, and then unravel.

The Common Whipping

The Palm-and-Needle Whipping

The Sailmaker's Whipping

The Snaked Whipping

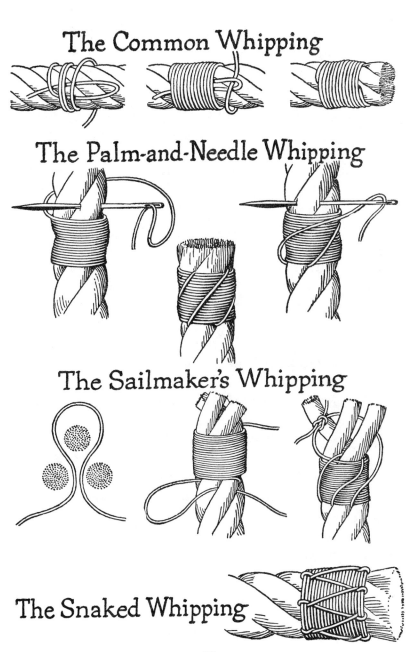

The Palm-and-Needle Whipping

This is the finest of all whippings, and although it takes a few minutes longer to put on than other types its superiority justifies the time that it requires. I have yet to see a whipping of this kind come off, even when many of the turns were cut or chafed through. As its name implies a sail needle and a sewing palm are employed, and the sail twine is put on *doubled*.

Wax a doubled length of twine and take a couple of stitches through a strand of the rope to anchor the end, and then put on the required number of turns evenly and snugly. Thrust the needle through the middle of a strand, emerging at the contline, and then *worm* the whipping back to the left side and thrust the needle through the next strand beyond. Now pull the twine up tightly and worm it back to the right side of the whipping, thrust the needle through the next strand and pull it tight. Finally, worm back to the left side again and again stitch through the strand and tighten.

You can now take a couple of short stitches through the strand to anchor the twine and cut it off close, for the whipping is complete. However, for a really good job you should continue around the rope a second time, thus *doubling* the worming. This gives additional protection from wear and chafe, and in my opinion makes a much better looking whipping.

The Sailmaker's Whipping

Authorities on seamanship seem to be in the dark as to the origin of this whipping, and in fact do not give it a name. Since the only reference naming it that I have been able to unearth calls it the *Sailmaker's Whipping*, I am using it here with reservations. Since it is nothing more than an *imitation Palm-and-Needle Whipping*, I can't conceive a sailmaker using it when he's constantly wearing a sewing palm and has needles galore by his side!

Actually it is a very useful type of whipping which seems to be supplanting its predecessor, and the reason for its popularity is that the palm and needle are not required. It can be used wherever you happen to be standing at the moment, without the necessity of dropping everything to go fetch your ditty bag.

The rope end is first carefully unlaid two or three inches. Then make a loose loop near the end of your waxed twine and place it over one strand, with the short end and the working end brought out between the other two strands. Be sure the loop is left several inches long. Then lay up the three strands again, twisting each strand to its original lay as you do so.

Now put on the required number of turns with the working end of the twine and then bring the loop up over the top of the strand that it encircles. Pull hard on the *starting* end, which draws up the loop and tightens the worming. Then worm the same end to the top and reef-knot it to the working end in the heart of the rope between the strands. Trim off the rope end and the whipping is completed.

Thus you have a secure whipping that is wormed over the turns like the Palm-and-Needle type, and except for the reef-knot which is hidden between the strands it would be hard to distinguish between the two types of whippings.

The Snaked Whipping

The taking of numerous hitches across the turns of a whipping transversely is called *snaking*. Its purpose is to provide the maximum protection against chafing of the turns, and is used primarily on ropes of large size, from ¾ inch diameter up. Aside from its practical value it is very decorative and gives a handsome finish to a rope end.

Snaking is always applied over a *Common Whipping* with a separate length of *doubled* sail twine or marline and a sail needle. After stitching through a strand to anchor the end, take a hitch about the *two outside turns* of the whipping, alternately across the turns to the right and left as shown. Secure the end with a stitch through the strand to anchor it.

VIII

Seizings

There is an old saying, that "when a sailor sews on a button it is on for the life of the garment." It is an adage worth remembering, for it typifies the competence, the craftsmanship and the painstaking care with which the sailor of old approached the task at hand. With him nothing was ever "good enough," it had to be *right*. In the practice of his skills he was dominated by tradition —everything had to be done a certain way, just as it had been done long before his time. Why? Well, because thousands of sailors in thousands of ships long forgotten, had discovered that it was the *best* way. *Security* was ever their goal, for there could be no compromise with craftsmanship where their lives and the safety of their ships were concerned.

This strict adherence to tradition would be found even in so simple a thing as a seizing, and were you to board a hundred ships in the days of sail you would find the seizings to be identical. So even today the yachtsman and the professional rigger clap on a seizing in the same manner, because no one has been able to devise a better way.

The commonest use for a seizing today is to form an eye in a rope, where splicing is either impractical or undesirable. Its greatest value is where the eye is made around a thimble, for a seizing will draw the throat or neck of the eye much closer and tighter to the thimble than a splice. A seizing must be used to put an eye in braided rope, for although it is possible to splice braided material few persons would have the interest to devote the time to it that it requires.

Seizings are made with tarred marline, which is two-strand hemp, left laid. The traditional way of starting a seizing is with an *eye-splice* in the end of the marline. The strands are only tucked once, as shown in the illustration, and the ends are left long and buried under the first few turns of the seizing. Many men, however, have large fingers and small patience, and splicing stuff as small as marline might be rather awkward. For them the *tucked eye* is recommended. The marline is simply twisted a bit to unlay it and the end is tucked through the strands a few times as shown.

The most commonly used seizing is the *Round Seizing*. It has two layers of turns, one superimposed on the other. After the first layer or row has been put on, a second row, called *riding turns* are applied and they are *two* less in number.

For a seizing of a less permanent nature the *riding turns* are omitted. This is known as a *Flat Seizing*.

The turns of a seizing are always taken *against* the lay of the rope, and you work *toward* the eye. Having positioned the rope, the marline is looped around the two parts by passing the working end through the tucked or

The Marline Eye

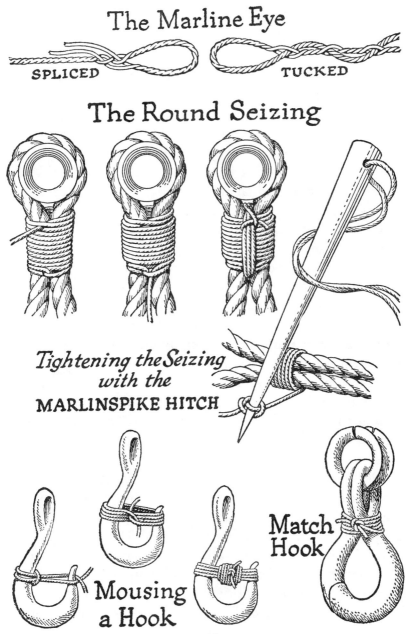

SPLICED   TUCKED

The Round Seizing

*Tightening the Seizing
with the*
MARLINSPIKE HITCH

Match
Hook

Mousing
a Hook

spliced eye. Needless to say the turns are now taken close together and as tightly as possible. Sufficient tension can rarely be had by the hands alone, and here is where the marlinspike comes in handy.

After every *third turn* heave taut on the seizing by using the marlinspike as a lever with a *marlinspike hitch* about the point, as shown in the illustration. When ten or twelve turns have been put on, a *single hitch* is taken to hold the gain, and then the *riding turns* are started. *Riding turns* should be put on only hand taut, for if heaved on with the spike there is danger of forcing them down into the lower set of turns. As before stated the riding turns should be two less in number than the lower turns. With the last turn the end is passed from back to front, between the two ropes and through the eye splice or tucked eye. Finally, two or three *crossing turns* are taken about the seizing, hauled as taut as possible and finished off with a single hitch.

With the exception of minor variations of no particular importance, this is the traditional form of *Round Seizing* in use for over 300 years, and if *properly done* there is small chance of it ever slipping, even after severe abuse.

Very often you will encounter deck blocks, or halyard blocks in gaff-rigged yachts, that are fitted with hooks instead of shackles. To prevent the hooks from unshipping, a different type of seizing, called a *Mousing*, is required. To *mouse* a hook a length of marline is *doubled* and secured to the *back* of the hook with a *sling hitch* as shown. The two strands or parts are then separated and brought around the *bill* of the hook on opposite sides.

After eight to ten turns have been taken with each, they are crossed in the center, and working outward with each part a number of *crossing* or *frapping* turns are taken tightly; then a set of *riding turns* back to the center where it is finished off with a *square* or *reef knot.*

Blocks are also sometimes fitted with what are variously known as *match hooks* or *sister hooks.* Here, too, a seizing is needed to prevent the two halves of the hook from separating and thus unshipping the block. Because there is no great strain imposed on it, a *Flat Seizing* finished off with a square knot is all that is required.

The *principles* of the seizings herein described may be employed in diverse ways. You will no doubt recognize their application in *lashings* of various kinds, where the turns bear the strains and the *crossing turns,* with or without *riders,* serve to tighten up the parts and hold them in position.

IX

Belaying, Coiling and Stowing

If there is one virtue necessary to the safe and efficient operation of a yacht it is *orderliness*—the habit of keeping things in their proper places and maintaining them in a shipshape condition, ready for use whenever needed. Orderliness is a habit hard come by, and it can be obtained only by strict, personal discipline and constant vigilance. Little details often seem inconsequential if considered separately, and it is all too easy to neglect them; but the total effect is cumulative and before you realize it you have an ill-kept, disordered ship where everything seems to go wrong.

One of the commonest causes of trouble is loose gear strewn about the deck, ready to trip the unwary and getting a-foul of everything that moves, and rope is the most serious offender. I know of but few things more dangerous to life, limb and the pursuit of happiness aboard a yacht than a fouled rope, whether it be sheet, halyard or cable. The only preventatives are to establish a procedure in the handling and use of rope in accordance with a few simple rules, and to make certain that they are followed, not only by yourself but by every member of your crew. Nor is this a temporary state of affairs. Throughout his entire life afloat the competent skipper is continually alert for the first sign of a rope that has become unclear.

Herewith are a few fundamental procedures that I have learned the hard way, by years of experience and observation, and by many painful errors. I do not claim that they are the best, for different sailors have different ways of achieving the same ends, but they answer my needs very satisfactorily.

To *belay* a sheet or halyard is to secure it to a cleat or belaying pin by taking a round turn and several S turns about it. To *make fast* is to further secure it by adding a *single hitch* over the belaying turns. I have noticed that many yachtsmen fail to make this distinction, apparently believing that *belay* and *make fast* have the same meaning.

One small detail, and a mighty important one, is that the first turn about a cleat or pin should be a *round turn,* the line making a complete circuit before crossing over with the S-turns. Thus when the S-turns are cast off you have a complete turn and easy friction for snubbing the rope, or easing it out gently and smoothly. Making the initial turn an S-turn is a lubberly practice, and the hapless offender should be put in irons for the duration of the voyage!

It is important that when a hitch is used to make fast a line over a cleat, the hitch must be thrown so that the working end of the line lies beside and not over the top turn on the cleat.

Now all this may sound, and probably is elementary,

but the only way to do so simple a thing as this is the *right way,* sailor-fashion, and it's surprising how many fool innovations you'll encounter. I remember an incident aboard a 35 foot sloop during a race in heavy weather. In a hard thrash to windward the mainsheet suddenly went by the run and the heavy boom fetched up against the backstay and broke in half. The nitwit who was supposed to be tending the mainsheet had taken three *round turns* about the cleat and nothing more, not even bothering to hold the sheet in his hand. Then there are those who reason that if a single hitch is secure two or three must be even better, and this can lead to trouble because the sheet or halyard can't be cast off quickly enough.

You will notice in the first illustration that the *lead* of the sheet or halyard is at an angle to the cleat, whether on the right side or the left. Many boat builders install cleats *in line* with the lead, which is incorrect, and if your yacht is so equipped by all means shift the cleats. The reason the angle is important is that you should be able to *snub* a sheet, that is, to take off all but one or two of the S turns and ease the sheet out gradually, the remaining turns acting as a brake and relieving the strain. When the cleat is in line with the lead the turns are jammed between the cleat and the standing part, which results in severe chafing and excessive friction, and the sheet will run out in a series of jerks. When an angle of about 10 degrees is obtained the sheet runs smoothly, with a minimum of wear.

After many unpleasant and in some cases hazardous experiences in belaying and making fast I have made

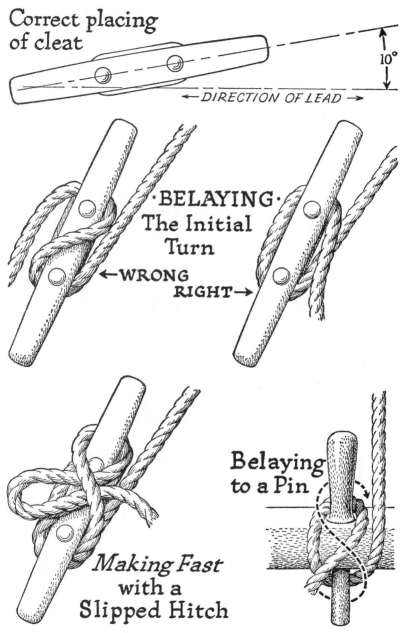

Correct placing of cleat

10°

←DIRECTION OF LEAD→

·BELAYING·
The Initial
Turn

←WRONG

RIGHT→

Making Fast
with a
Slipped Hitch

Belaying
to a Pin

71

a rule to which I adhere religiously: *never make fast a sheet*. I generally make fast my halyards, for I want them to stay where I put them, but under no circumstance will I add that single hitch to a belayed sheet. It is a dangerous practice, and entirely unnecessary.

Yachtsmen are divided into two groups on this point, the deep draft, or keel men, who belay and make fast their sheets come hell or high water, and the shoal draft or centerboard men who never make fast, and belay as little as possible. Since most of my experience was acquired in centerboard craft I obviously belong in the latter group. I have witnessed or have been a party to many capsizings and swampings, a few of which were the result of lugging too much sail, but the majority of them were caused by inability to cast off and slack sheets quickly enough, and that single hitch on top of the belaying turns was generally responsible.

A sheet should be ready for slacking or trimming at a moment's notice, which in turn means casting it off in the shortest possible time, and a single hitch takes *too much* of that time. Furthermore it is entirely unnecessary, for if enough turns are taken in belaying the sheet will not slip, and turns can be cast off quicker than a hitch.

However, in all fairness I should point out a compromise by which you may belay and make fast a sheet fairly safely. The illustration shows how a *slipped turn* may be used in place of the single hitch. It is just as secure and can be cast off by a quick tug on the sheet. Its weakness lies in the fact that it can be cast off accidentally, and I find it awkward to put it on with one hand.

The last illustration shows how to belay to a belaying pin and no comment is necessary as the method is the same as is employed with a cleat. Here, however, *security* is the important thing, and as many turns are taken as the pin will comfortably hold. It is made fast with the single hitch, in the case of halyards, because heavy seas coming aboard could easily loosen or cast off the turns.

Immediately after belaying a sheet or halyard the inactive working part should be coiled and disposed of in a manner which will best prevent its becoming fouled. Halyards must be treated differently from sheets. Once a sail is set the halyard remains belayed until the sail is taken in; therefore the coil may be secured in a fixed position directly to the cleat or pin to which it is belayed.

Let us assume that the halyard is belayed *above the deck,* either to a cleat on the mast or a belaying pin in a pin rail. This is an ideal arrangement, for the coil can be hung from the cleat or pin, out of the way of everything with the deck clear and uncluttered. The illustration shows clearly the best method of securing the coil. The turns of the coil are always started *next to the cleat or pin* and are concluded at the end of the rope. Now hold the coil in your left hand and with the right pull the bight of the standing part through the coil, twist it to the *left,* or against the lay, and slip it over the pin or the upper horn of the cleat. Thus the coil is most secure, the turns cannot possibly be disturbed, and you know that in heavy weather you will not find the coil lying in the lee scuppers hopelessly fouled. When ready to cast off the halyard, slip the bight off the pin and drop the coil on the deck, face down. It is then ready to run, free and clear.

In coiling sheets or halyards *never* start with the bitter end for this causes kinks. A coil should be so made that the bitter end is a little longer than the coil and will

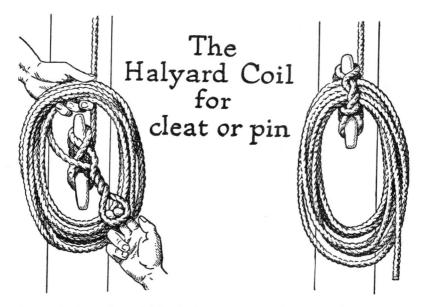

The Halyard Coil for cleat or pin

hang below it, which helps prevent it from fouling in the turns.

If the halyard belays to a cleat on the deck or cabin top the above method cannot be used. Instead I recommend that shown in the next illustration. It is actually a *sea gasket* coil used in the days of the square-riggers. The coil is started about 2 feet from the cleat. After the coil has been made four or five frapping turns are taken with the standing part about the upper part of the coil.

Then a bight of the standing part is pulled through the coil above the turns and looped back over the head of the coil snugly. Thus the coil is held together and neatly tethered to the cleat.

Sheet coils cannot be secured because they must at all times be free to run. As I stated before there is a constant danger of sheets becoming kinked, snarled or fouled. Since they are generally led to the cockpit the surplus rope is usually coiled and dropped to the floor, or on the deck close by. Guests have an annoying and dangerous habit of sitting or standing on the coil, and careless crew members will often snag their feet in the turns. Outside of standing guard over the coil with a gun, there is no known way to keep your sheet free and clear other than to be eternally vigilant, and to recoil and overhaul them the instant they become unclear.

Anchor cables present a different set of problems. Like sheets and halyards they too must be at all times ready for use and free to run. Since a cable is generally carried on the forward deck there is a constant possibility of its being washed overboard or fouled by solid water coming aboard. The anchor itself should be securely lashed to something solid, preferably the bitts, bowsprit or mooring cleat. *All* lashings about the yacht should be secured with the *Slipped Reef Knot*.

A cable is too large to be coiled in the hand and so it is coiled down directly on the deck, starting next to the anchor. Make each turn slightly larger than the preceding one, because this makes it run more freely, and keep the coil as large as convenient to allow for free circulation of air about the parts. Now capsize the coil carefully,

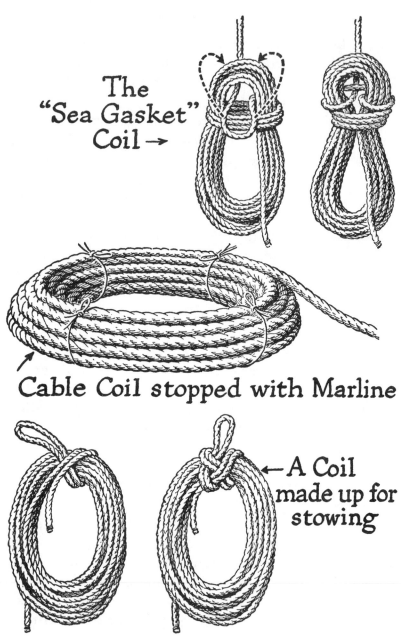

The "Sea Gasket" Coil →

Cable Coil stopped with Marline

← A Coil made up for stowing

rearranging any turn that is out of line, and put on four stops of marline or cotton line, tying each with a Slipped Reef Knot for ease in casting off, as shown in the illustration.

The stowage of inactive coils below deck is a detail which deserves considerable thought and should be done in a seamanlike manner. In general terms, spare gear should be stowed in a well ventilated and accessible place. In a small yacht this is somewhat of a problem because there is so little available space; but it should be remembered that this gear is necessary to the working of the ship, and should therefore be given preference over things of lesser importance.

In stowing, the coils should be hung up rather than laid flat with one piled on the other, not only for accessibility but to keep them untangled. The last illustration shows a neat and handy way of making up a coil for hanging. A bight is formed near the end and a hitch is taken tightly about the head of the coil to the right, then another hitch is taken to the left. It resembles a clove hitch but is another thing entirely. This makes a neat, secure coil that will withstand considerable handling, and furnishes a loop for hanging it up.

X

The Service of Wire and Rope

Before the introduction of wire rope all standing rigging was tarred hemp, generally 4-strand, and was set up with deadeyes and lanyards. Being subjected to constant chafe of yards and sails, and needing some sort of protection from the elements to combat excessive stretching and rot, shrouds and stays were always *wormed, parcelled* and *served* throughout their length.

Worming is the laying in of small-stuff between the strands to fill the spaces which would otherwise hold moisture and cause rot, and to make the surface of the rope smoother. *Parcelling* consists of narrow strips of old canvas soaked with rigging tar wrapped about the rope spirally with the lay, the edges overlapping, to prevent moisture from entering the rope. The rope is *served* after parcelling by covering it with tightly-wound, close turns of marline or hemp small-stuff, *against* the lay. It is then heavily tarred to make it waterproof, and maintenance consists of replacement of chafed sections and regular, periodic re-tarring.

After service, the rope is considerably stiffer, slightly stronger, completely waterproof, and its normal life is extended beyond measure. Indeed, many an American whaleship still carried her original hempen shrouds and stays a whole generation or more after wire rope was universally adopted. Whalers were noted for their longevity, and the rigging that we now consider primitive did in fact last as long as the ship.

When iron wire superseded hemp, worming was of course no longer necessary; but parcelling and serving and tarring were still required to prevent rust, chafe and wear. Galvanizing merely delayed for a short while the inevitable corrosive effect of salt water. How well the service of wire fulfilled its purpose was amply demonstrated to me a few years ago. I had fallen heir to the standing rigging and assorted gear from an oyster sloop which was built in 1886 and dismantled after some 60 years of hard usage. Her shrouds were half-inch iron wire, parcelled and served throughout their length and set up with deadeyes and lanyards.

Out of curiosity I removed the tar-stiffened marline and canvas from the lower end of one of the shrouds, and to my surprise the wire beneath was entirely free from rust and as bright and clean as new. It was hard to believe, that after 60 years of exposure to the elements and continual drenching in salt water there was no deterioration, but from that same wire I made two bowsprit shrouds which now grace my *Morning Star,* then a-building!

Now you may well say: "That's all very interesting, but I can't see where this ancient art of the rigger from a forgotten era has any value aboard my very modern 30 foot cutter, rigged from stem to stern with stainless steel and swaged-on fittings." Well, I'll admit it is a debatable point and not a very critical issue, but nevertheless I am aggressively on the affirmative side.

To begin with, yachts that lie to a buoyed mooring often have a wire mooring pennant, and without the protection afforded by serving or other covering the bare wire can do considerable damage to the hull. Parcelling and serving build up the diameter and present a softer surface at the point of contact. Many comparatively small cruising yachts are fitted with permanently-rigged lifelines of stainless wire rope, often of small diameter. They should be served throughout their length to give a better handhold and to lessen the chance of bodily injury if one should be thrown into them.

Bowsprit shrouds and footropes most certainly should be served over to reduce the possibility of slipping and to make them easier on the feet. Standing on ¼ inch wire in one's bare feet while taking in headsails is anything but fun, but when you build it up to ½ inch by parcelling and serving you get sure footing, and it's easier to stand on.

Stainless steel wire rope is notoriously slippery, not only to grab hold of but to secure a line to. In my opinion all such shrouds and backstays should be parcelled and served to a height of 5 or 6 feet above the deck for this reason. It increases the bulk of the wire to a comfortable degree and gives a textured surface more suitable for the hitching on of flag halyards, temporary life lines and lashings.

Eye splices in wire should always be served over, not

only about the splice itself but around the entire eye. Many yachts, particularly those that are gaff-rigged, have wire sheet and halyard bridles, blockstraps and slings, all of which are customarily served.

So I think it is quite evident that sufficient need for this ancient art still exists to justify the modern yachtsman's learning the proper methods involved in its practice.

Parcelling as done in olden times, by cutting up strips of canvas and soaking them in tar, is exceedingly messy and more appropriate for a fishing vessel than a fine yacht. Fortunately a far superior substitute may be had in common electrician's friction tape, of which there are two kinds—cloth and rubber. Under no circumstances should rubber tape be used, as the sulphuric acid content of rubber could in time attack the wire. The cloth tape, laid on tightly in overlapping turns makes perfect parcelling for wire, as the waterproof adhesive with which it is impregnated completely fills the interstices between the individual strands when squeezed by the pressure of the serving.

The old saying, "worm and parcel *with* the lay, turn and serve the *other* way," should be strictly adhered to. The only exception is when the parceling is used without serving, as for chafing gear on Manila, in which it should be applied against the lay.

It is impossible to apply serving with the hands alone and expect a decent job. The marline will cut your hands long before the proper tension can be reached. A tool called a *serving mallet* is employed, and since it is generally a homemade article I have shown one here of a size suitable for the amateur yachtsman, with enough dimensions to make his own.

Under ideal conditions the wire rope to be served is secured at each end breast-high and hauled taut with a tackle, being so anchored that it cannot turn or twist. The marline is then secured with a *clove hitch* and a few turns are made with the hands alone. The mallet is now placed in position as shown in the illustration, with one turn about the *leading* side of the mallet head, two turns about the *following* side, and one turn about the handle itself. Grasping the handle and rotating the tool about the wire lays on the marline in very close turns and exceedingly tight.

The tension of the marline is achieved by the friction on the head and the handle, and is easily controlled. Too few turns give no tension at all, and too many will break the marline. The tighter you grasp the handle and the marline wound about it the greater the friction. With proper tension the tool sets up a continuous squealing and the tar or oil will be squeezed out to the surface of the marline. So great is the leverage obtained with the serving mallet that it takes a little adjustment to keep just under the breaking point of the marline. When you are all set the tool may be literally spun around the rope rapidly, and with the ambrosial smell of tar in your nostrils and the high-pitched squeal of the marline providing the background music it is a most pleasant task.

For serving eyes, and for small jobs where the serving mallet with the spool might be cumbersome, the *serving*

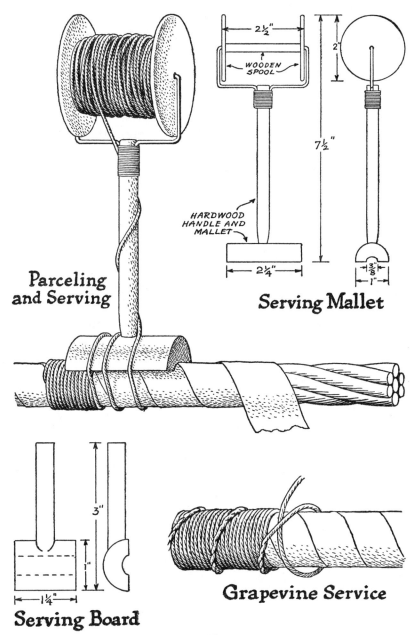

Parceling and Serving

Serving Mallet

WOODEN SPOOL

2½"

2"

7½"

HARDWOOD HANDLE AND MALLET

2¼"

3/8"

1"

Serving Board

3"

1"

1¼"

Grapevine Service

83

board comes in handy. It is basically the same except that the handle, which is rarely more than 3 inches long, is on the side instead of the top. However, with this tool a helper is needed to pass the ball of marline around the rope or wire since it has no spool to hold it.

After wire rope has been served it should be painted or varnished to make it waterproof. Spar varnish, black asphaltum or white yacht paint may be used, as your fancy dictates, and each year at fitting-out time it should be refinished.

Iron stanchions and handrails are often served over for the sake of appearance. A very handsome and decorative effect may be had by the use of *grapevine service,* which is put on by hand and painted over. As will be seen from the illustration it is nothing more than a series of hitches, all taken in the same direction and hauled as taut as the hands will permit. Of course it takes considerably longer than common serving, but since it is the uncommon we are striving for, who cares? Spending seventy-five dollars' worth of one's time piddling around with a piece of string pays the kind of dividends not measurable in coin of the realm.

XI

Hand Sewing and Canvaswork

The ancient art of sewing with the palm and sail needle is perhaps the most difficult for the amateur yachtsman to master. To begin with there are but few books which cover the subject adequately and specific information is not within easy reach of the average person. Furthermore it is an art that requires countless hours of tedious practice to achieve even a moderate degree of proficiency. Any sailmaker will tell you that he had to serve a long apprenticeship learning to use the tools of his craft before he was initiated into the mysteries of cutting a sail.

Lest this appear to be an attempt to dissuade you from even trying, let me hasten to add that any amateur of average intelligence can learn very quickly to sew a simple seam in canvas that will be reasonably straight, smooth and secure, often on the first attempt. But you must not be discouraged because the quality of your work is greatly inferior to that of the professional sailmaker. All that is required is that you have a fundamental knowledge of tools and methods, and enough skill to meet the needs of the average small yacht.

Of course, the first use for the palm-and-needle that

comes to mind is the emergency repair of torn sails. But there are also canvas covers of all kinds to make or repair, as well as various useful articles of ship's gear. Winter covers invariably suffer storm damage and require patching or mending. Sailmakers are not found at every mooring, nor can they be always had as willing shipmates, and if you can handle the palm-and-needle with a fair degree of skill you are just that much nearer self-sufficiency.

Before getting into the methods employed in hand sewing it would be advisable to learn something about the tools of the craft, not only as a guide in purchasing them but also for a better understanding of their use.

The *Sewing Palm* is nothing more than a seagoing thimble, used to push the needle through the canvas. Made of heavy leather and rawhide, it goes over your whole hand with a hole for your thumb and a strap across the back to keep it in place. The business part of it is a small chunk of iron supported by rawhide just below the thumb, with numerous indentations in which you seat the needle. Apparently all sailmakers are right-handed, for I have never seen a left-handed palm outside of a museum.

When new, a palm is as stiff as a board and as hard to break in as a new pair of brogans. Some soak their palm in water and wear it until it is softened up, but I have found it easier to soak it in neatsfoot oil and knead it with the hands until it is soft and pliable. It must fit your hand comfortably or it is useless, and since palms do not come in sizes it must be adjusted as required.

The leather around the thumb hole and the strap

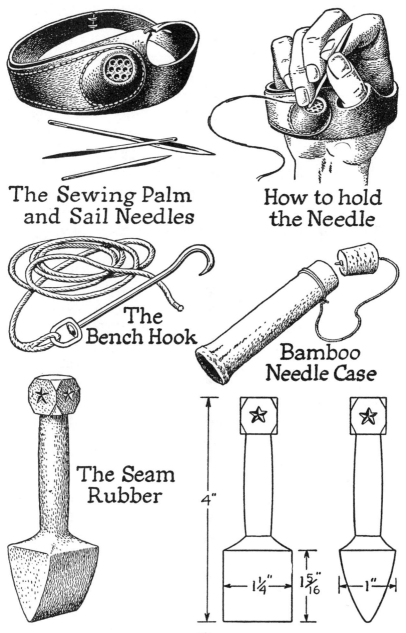

The Sewing Palm
and Sail Needles

How to hold
the Needle

The
Bench Hook

Bamboo
Needle Case

The Seam
Rubber

4"

1¼"

1 5/16"

1"

across the back of the hand are secured with a seizing of twine—cheap palms are fastened with a metal clip and are very inferior tools. By means of this seizing you can tighten up or slacken the palm to fit. It is important that you have a snug fit around the thumb, but the back strap should be loose enough to barely touch the hand. Examine the iron and see if enough working area is exposed—oftentimes you will find it nearly covered by the rawhide and it is then necessary to enlarge the hole by cutting or burning it.

The *Sailmaker's Needle* is triangular in section, tapering to a full round near the eye. Its peculiar shape is designed to suit the heavy material in which it is used. As it enters the canvas it gently parts the fibers with a minimum of effort, and as it is withdrawn the hole closes up and grips the thread. If you were to push a round needle of the same diameter into the same canvas you would notice that it meets with greater resistance, and the friction set up requires far more power to force it through.

The finest needles are made by Wm. Smith & Son, England, and are so marked. You will find others marked "Jas. Smith & Sons, England," and "Showell, England." The first named have what are known as "reduced edges," which means that the edges of the triangular section are noticeably rounded, whereas the latter two makes are sharp of edge and harder on the fingers and the canvas.

The size of the needle is designated by number, the lower the number the larger the needle. The smallest size you will ever need is No. 17, a scant 2 inches long and suitable only for light weight material such as spinnaker cloth. The heavier the canvas the larger the needle, and it is difficult to give specific recommendations. I find that most of the time I am using a No. 15 or 14, and I always have a full assortment in my ditty bag, including a few large enough to take marline.

Some sort of needle case is really necessary, for the ever-present dampness will otherwise rust your needles very quickly. One easy solution is to use a 6 inch section of bamboo from a discarded fishing pole, with a cork in each end and an oil-soaked bit of absorbant cotton inside. My own was ingeniously made by a whaleman in 1850 from the wing bone of an albatross, the ends neatly plugged with wood.

Sail Twine for sewing had best be obtained from a sailmaker. When you ask for sail twine in most marine supply stores you are generally handed a ball of fuzzy stuff that looks like, and I suspect often is grocery string. Good sail twine is smooth and strong—when well-waxed it will cut your hand before it breaks. It is put up in spools, in three sizes—fine, medium and heavy. You should have one of each.

The sailmaker never sews without first waxing his twine with beeswax. It makes the twine cling to the canvas, prevents it from snarling or looping and adds to its strength. Good beeswax is easy to obtain, and is sticky and dark in color. Poor beeswax is hard and crumbly and light in color. Many sailmakers cook up their own, adding various things such as grease to get the preferred consistency.

A *Bench Hook* is an absolute must. It takes the place

of an extra hand to hold the canvas in place on your lap. Without it you would draw the material up into a bunch every time you tried to take a stitch. It is hooked into a completed seam or the body of the cloth right over your right leg, for you always sew away from it to the left. The lanyard of the hook is secured to the end of your bench or seat. I have seen many amateurs attempt to sew without a bench hook, and they invariably botched the job.

The *Seam Rubber* I have here illustrated is an ancient tool of the sailmaker used for creasing a fold in canvas or to smooth out a completed seam. While not an absolute necessity, it is a very handy tool to have in your sewing kit. Since it is a homemade article and cannot be obtained otherwise, I have included dimensions for making your own. Many old seam rubbers for use on shipboard were made of whale ivory or bone, but any hard, close-grained wood will do. When folding the edge of canvas over for a seam, a sharp, straight crease can be made by running the rubber back and forth, bearing down hard as you do so.

Except for your sheath knife, marlinspike and fid, that about covers the tools required for hand sewing. While they can be assembled piecemeal if you so desire, excellent kits may be had from Ratsey & Lapthorn, Inc., City Island, N.Y. They were designed expressly for the amateur yachtsman, and since their makers are sailmakers of repute you can be assured that they are of excellent quality.

All canvas is made with a colored marking thread an inch or more from the selvage edge, parallel to it. This is a guide for overlapping two pieces of material to make a seam. However, when making a seam with a *cut edge* instead of a selvage, the raw edge must first be turned under ¼ inch to eliminate the unsightly fraying that would otherwise occur.

The stitch used in seaming is called the *flat stitch,* and it is made by first picking up a bight of the lower cloth right alongside of the lapped edge and then coming up through the lap as close to the edge as you comfortably can without danger of the stitch pulling out. You always sew with the edge of the *upper* cloth facing *away* from you and progress from right to left. That means that you are pushing the needle diagonally toward you to the left.

Before sewing can be actually started it is vitally important that you know how to hold and operate the palm and needle. In this lies the real secret to successful sewing, and in this the uninstructed beginner inevitably goes haywire.

If you will study the accompanying illustration you will see that the needle is held between the thumb and forefinger *close to the point,* and the third finger keeps the needle seated in the iron. Now with the needle held in this manner you sew with the hand held practically flat to the canvas, and the needle should be held seated in the iron at all times except when catching hold of it when the point emerges from the canvas. The sailmaker actually inserts and withdraws the needle in one continual motion—in fact he hardly appears to let go of the needle at all. He pushes the needle through with the whole arm rather than with a wrist motion, and at the

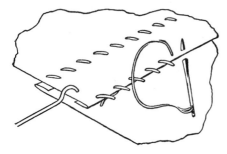

The Flat Seam The Round Seam

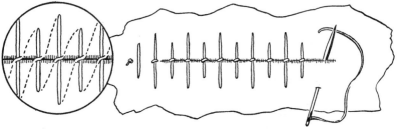

The Herringbone Darning Stitch

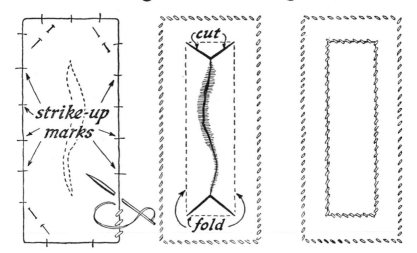

strike-up marks

cut

fold

Applying a Patch

end of a long day it is his shoulder that is tired, which is an indication that it has been doing all the work.

By way of comparison notice how an uninformed amateur sews. He picks up the needle and pushes it part way through with his fingers and then, remembering what the palm is for, he brings the iron up to the needle and gives a mighty shove with his hand outspread! The needle wobbles about precariously as if uncertain just where to go, and more than likely he harpoons himself in the right leg. I know that this is a typical performance because I did it many times before learning the correct way.

You'll not acquire the professional technique on your first attempt, nor even with a month of practice, but it is something to shoot for. I am sure you will then envy the effortless rhythm of the professional sailmaker as he literally walks down a seam.

Since you always work with the material over your lap there is a tendency to sew the canvas to your trousers. This can be avoided by first laying a piece of heavy, stiff canvas across your knees. Then when the needle goes through your work you will hear a definite "tick" sound as the point hits the heavy canvas, a signal to bring the needle up again.

But to get on with our sewing. Thread your needle and pull the twine through until you have about an arm's length doubled. Strip it across the beeswax a couple of times and then roll it down your thigh with the flat of your hand to give it a twist or lay. With a yard or so of canvas to practice upon, turn an edge over, crease it down to form a hem, and hook your bench hook into it by your right leg. Now try your first stitch, and draw the thread through except for about an inch. This end is pushed ahead of the first stitch under the seam and the next stitch is then taken right over it. Thus the end of the thread is enclosed in the line of stitches to anchor it, in lieu of a knot. The professional never knots the end of his thread as does the seamstress, for it makes a hard lump in the seam and is unnecessary.

Your stitches should be made in a straight line and as evenly as possible. Draw a pencil guide line if you desire. The spacing of the stitches depends upon the weight of the cloth—the lighter the material the closer and smaller the stitches. There is a rule for this that works out very well, and it is 10 stitches to the length of the needle. Thus with a No. 15 needle, which is 2½ inches long, you would take 10 stitches to every 2½ inches of seam, and they would be ¼ inch apart.

Do not draw up the stitches too tightly or you will unduly pucker the seam. Just use enough tension to sink the thread into the cloth slightly, and strive for even tension throughout. Your main goal should be even, straight stitches exactly alike in every respect. As you progress along the seam, keep shifting the bench hook ahead to bring your work in front of you. Rubbing the finished seam down with the seam rubber smooths it down and evens up the tension.

In addition to the flat seam we have been discussing there is the *round seam,* used only where the seam forms an *edge* of the canvas. As will be seen in the illustration it is an "over and over" stitch. One use for it which comes to mind is in the repair of a sail, where a tear extends right through the leech. In applying a patch the *round seam* is used along the leech and the *flat seam* on the rest of the patch.

Every sailing yacht sooner or later suffers torn sails. I am not going into the reasons for sail damage, for they are many, but it is imperative that you know how to make both temporary and permanent repairs on the spot. A little tear scarcely 3 inches long can quickly grow into a rip clean across the sail if not caught in time. Here the proverbial "stitch in time" may not only save nine, but it may prevent the whole sail from being damaged beyond repair.

The simplest form of sail repair is that universally employed by the teen-agers in the smaller racing craft, a crazy-quilt pattern of adhesive tape from the first-aid kit. While it apparently works successfully, it cannot be relied upon with any degree of confidence and had best be considered for what it is—a kid's ingenious trick.

For a simple straight-line tear in the body of the sail, the *round seam stitch* is often used—the two edges are brought together and sewn in the simple "over and over" manner. In fact, this is the only stitch that most beginners know. But I do not like it, nor would I ever recommend it. In the first place the *round seam stitch* gathers up the cloth from either side of the tear to such a degree that there is not only danger of the stitches pulling out, but the sail may be stretched permanently out of shape; particularly if the tear is in the vicinity of the leech.

The best form of darn for a straight tear is the *herring-bone stitch,* consisting of alternately long and short stitches, with a "hitch" in each stitch along the line of the tear. It is particularly good when the sail is old and weak. The illustration shows how it is done and I doubt if it is necessary to explain it.

It should be noted, however, that the stitches are started *beyond* the tear where they can be anchored in whole cloth. They are taken far enough back from the edges of the tear so that they will not pull through into the rip itself. Note also that the stitches should be made straight across, at right angles to the line of the tear. Always use a doubled sail twine and wax it well. Incidentally, it is impossible to wax your sail twine when it is wet, so keep it dry and do your waxing below decks, if you are working in wet weather.

While it is sometimes possible to darn a tear with the sail set and drawing, it is far better to lower away for the few minutes that it takes. *Never* draw up your stitches any more than is necessary to just bring the edges of the tear together. Remember you are not trying to make the sail hold water, or even wind—the sole object of your temporary darn is to prevent the tear from spreading, until such time as it is possible to mend it permanently with a proper patch.

In the three accompanying illustrations I have shown the professional way of applying a patch for a permanent repair. The patch should be made with the same weight and material as the sail itself, and for that reason when ordering new sails you should always request the sailmaker to give you some scraps of the material for use in making repairs.

Spread your sail out on a smooth, clean surface and

straighten it in the vicinity of the tear so that it lies flat and even. Let us suppose the tear is a straight one about 6 inches long. Cut a patch about 3 by 9 inches and turn the edges under 1/4 inch all around, creasing it down with your seam rubber. Placing it carefully over the tear so that the threads in the patch run the same way as those in the sail, pin it in position, trying not to wrinkle or pucker up the cloth. In lieu of pins do as the sailmakers do—use spare sail needles.

Now with a soft pencil make a series of marks across the edge of the patch onto the sail. These are called "strike-up" marks. As you sew these marks are lined up to prevent gathering up one cloth more than the other. Starting at the upper right corner, sew the patch on with the *flat seam stitch,* and try to keep the stitches evenly spaced. If necessary, draw a pencil line around the patch first, to enable you to sew in a straight line.

When the patch has been sewn on, turn the sail over and smooth it out. With your knife or scissors slit the *sail only* at the four "corners" of the tear and turn under all four sides, thus turning the ragged tear into a neat oblong opening. Crease it well with the seam rubber and sew the edges down with the same *flat seam stitch.* This completes the job and it should now look like the third illustration.

Not all tears are clean or straight, but the same method is used to apply a patch. With a three-cornered tear the patch would be L-shaped, and you might need one in the form of a T or an X. At any rate, for the sake of neatness keep the patch a simple right-angled shape if the nature of the tear permits.

When making canvas bags, covers of all sorts and awnings, some form of grommets or eyelets are required in the edges to take a drawstring or lashing. Ashore, the professional generally inserts brass grommets with a grommet-setting die. Few amateurs however are equipped to do this, and *worked eyelet holes* may be used instead. The only tools required are your palm, needle and marlinspike, plus a bit of marline and sail twine. In addition to their being very handsome, *worked eyelets* will never pull out of the canvas as brass grommets so often do.

Let us assume you are making a ditty bag and need eyelet holes of the proper size to take ⅛ inch cotton line. The first step is to make up some grommets of marline, ½ inch in diameter (see page 54). Next punch a hole in the canvas with your marlinspike where desired and ream it to about ¼ inch diameter. Place the marline grommet over the hole and draw a pencil line around it. With this line as a guide, and using a doubled length of well-waxed twine, proceed to sew the grommet to the canvas. The needle is stuck down at the far side of the grommet and up through the hole, and the stitches should be taken close enough together to completely hide the grommet.

Variations may be had in several ways. *Two* lengths of twine may be threaded in the needle at a time, thus making a "thread" of four parts which bulks larger and gives more body to the eye. Small galvanized iron rings are easily obtained and may be used in place of marline grommets, being particularly useful in heavy canvas covers.

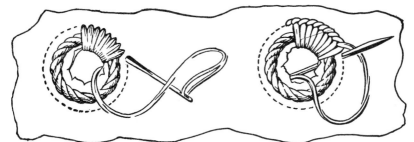

Common   **Hitched**

Worked Eyelets

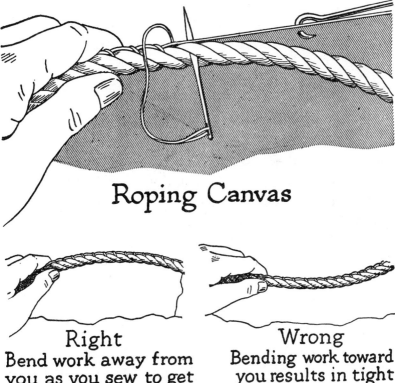

Roping Canvas

Right
Bend work away from
you as you sew to get
slack canvas and tight rope

Wrong
Bending work toward
you results in tight
canvas and slack rope

For a really beautiful job I recommend the use of the *hitched eyelet,* which I have here illustrated. It was often employed by the square-rigged sailor in the making of his personal gear and its counterpart may be found today in the "buttonholing" used by the seamstress.

In my remarks on the repairing of damaged sails I should have noted that there are limits beyond which the amateur yachtsman should not go—that where the damage is serious and extensive, the repairing had best be left to the professional sailmaker. Oftentimes a darn or a patch is out of the question and a whole cloth must be replaced, involving the re-roping of at least a part of the sail. Roping a sail is an art that requires a high degree of skill and long experience, and it is obviously not within the scope of the amateur.

Nevertheless roping is a necessary part of canvaswork and properly belongs in any discussion of the arts of the sailor. In the making of awnings, covers and various articles of gear you will need to know how to sew a bolt-rope to canvas, and while the skill required is nowhere near as exacting as in sailmaking, you should at least be familiar with the fundamental techniques employed.

Tarred hemp bolt-rope should always be used for roping, never cotton or manila, and ⅜ inch is about as large as you will ever need. Certain preparations must be made before it is ready for sewing. With one end made fast and the rope straightened out, hitch the other end to your marlinspike or a short stick and twist against the lay. The purpose is to partially unlay the rope and loosen it up throughout its length. Pull on it as you twist, and such is the nature of hemp that it will not spring back to its original lay when released.

When sufficiently loosened up the rope should be laid out on the floor or a level surface in a straight line, allowing it to assume its natural lay and without any twists or turns throughout its length. Then draw a straight line down the rope with a red or white crayon or chalk, being very careful to avoid rolling the rope as you go. This line serves as a guide in sewing to the canvas and prevents getting a twist to the rope which would otherwise be unnoticed.

In sewing on the bolt rope you work from left to right, with the rope on the near side of the canvas. Thus the needle goes first through the rope and then the canvas. The needle must go *under* the uppermost strand nearest the sail, and never *through* a strand. The proper size needle would be a No. 15 or 14, and if the point is dulled a bit on an oilstone there is less of a tendency to pick up or go through an adjacent strand.

Wax your doubled length of sail twine heavily and knot the end. Hook your bench hook into the canvas at your right and hold the rope to the canvas with the left hand, with the edge of the hem on the red line you previously marked for the purpose. Your needle should go through at practically a right angle to the rope, and the stitches should be drawn up just enough to sink the canvas a bit into the "contline"—the groove or space between the strands. This tends to gather up the canvas as you go along so that, in the case of an awning, the strain will come on the rope when it is set up taut instead of the canvas.

There is a fine relationship between the length of the rope and the canvas to which it is sewn that is difficult to attain. The beginner invariably gets what is known as a "slack" rope—that is, the rope actually measures longer than the canvas to which it is sewn. Unconsciously he bends the work toward his body or inwards, thus using up more rope than canvas. This results in a very poor job, and no matter how much the canvas is stretched the roped edge hangs in scallops and waves up and down in the breeze.

The sailmaker gets a tight rope and slack canvas by bending the work slightly *away* from himself, as I have illustrated, and by sinking the stitches as desired. It is to a large extent by this means that he builds the proper draft into a sail.

This is the technique to strive for—evenly spaced stitches, uniformly "sunk," and slack canvas rather than slack rope. The best means of acquiring it is by practice, and I suggest you take an odd piece of canvas with a hemmed edge at least four feet long and rope it. I found that it takes at least three or four feet to determine whether you are getting a tight or slack rope.

XII

Decorative Knots

When you speak of the arts of the sailor the average layman automatically thinks of decorative knots and fancy work, and more often than not looks upon such work as sailors' tricks or stunts. While it is true that decorative rope work is one of the oldest arts, it is not the only one by a long shot, nor is it so all-fired important.

In recent years we have had a plethora of books on knots, good, bad and indifferent, and in my opinion this art has been built up and promoted all out of proportion to its worth, while the many more important and perhaps less glamorous arts have been neglected or ignored completely. It is true that the average sailor of the old school generally had a complete repertoire of decorative knots and fancy rope work for it was a necessary part of his trade. But the fact that such work was either beautiful or decorative was secondary to its *usefulness*.

When he tied a Matthew Walker knot in a rope end it was not for entertainment, but to serve as a safe, efficient stopper knot. A 12-strand flat sennit that you and I would consider handsome was the only method he knew of making a gasket. It is fortunate indeed that such things *were* pleasing to the eye, but let's be rational in our thinking and keep the cart behind the horse where it belongs.

In this and the following chapter I propose to examine some of the decorative arts most useful to the yachtsman. In each instance their practical applications will be suggested, for in my choice of subjects *usefulness* has been the determining factor, and their inherent beauty should be considered in the light of an added bonus.

First on the agenda are the *Stopper Knots,* known variously as *Knob, Terminal* or *Lanyard Knots.* They are *permanent* knots tied in the end of a rope to raise a knob, and were generally used to prevent a rope from unreeving. The yachtsman, however, prefers the Figure-Eight Knot as a stopper since it can be readily untied, and it is therefore classed as a temporary knot. It was shown in the chapter on basic knots.

The first use for a permanent stopper knot that comes to mind is in finishing off a deck-bucket rope, to prevent the bitter end from slipping through the hand. The centerboard pennant likewise should have a stopper knot in the end to prevent it from unreeving. Manropes, tiller yoke-ropes, rope handles and bell pulls are other applications. Once you have mastered these knots your natural pride in your newly acquired skill will assert itself, and you'll soon be looking for and finding new uses for them.

I would like to emphasize right here, that in tying these or *any* knots where it is necessary to unlay the strands of a rope end you should first clap on a temporary seizing or stopping at the point to which you intend to unlay; likewise each strand end should be stopped before commencing the knot. The Constrictor Knot makes the best stopping I know of, it is quickly tied and never loosens.

The Wall Knot

This knot is rarely used by itself, as a stopper, but is a component part of many more elaborate ones. It is employed in making certain sennits, and in rope fenders. Although it is so simple it hardly needs describing, you will note in the illustration that each strand is passed around its neighbor on the right, *counterclockwise,* and that the strand ends emerge from the top of the knot.

The Crown Knot

This knot is the exact reverse of the Wall Knot, and the strands emerge from the bottom. You wall *up,* and you crown *down.* Peculiarly enough, if you turn either knot upside down it becomes the *other.* The Wall, like the Crown Knot, is rarely used alone; it is used in sennit and fender making, and together they form the basis of other knots.

Moving also counterclockwise, each strand crosses *over* the next strand ahead, and is enclosed in its bight.

The Wall-and-Crown Knot

First tie a wall and then superimpose a crown upon it. By combining the two you achieve more of a knob-like effect than either would give if used separately. But it still doesn't bulk up enough to be of practical use, and if the strand ends were cut off they would soon loosen and become un-tucked. Therefore the next logical step is to *double* the knot, thus forming a substantial knob knot called

The Manrope Knot

You will often hear this called the *Tack Knot,* or the Doubled Wall and Crown, the various names being derived from its application, and the disposition of the strand ends. This is perhaps the best known of all knob knots and the most widely used. Among experts it is considered very elementary, in the category of "fancy" knots, but despite its simplicity it is very neat and symmetrical, and every yachtsman should know and use it.

To tie the Manrope Knot, first make the single Wall-and-Crown, but *do not* pull it up taut—keep it loose and open. Referring to the first illustration, each strand in turn must be passed around and outside of its own part, as shown by the dotted arrow. When all 3 strands have been so passed you will have *doubled* the *Wall Knot,* and it should look like the second illustration.

Now each strand, always working counterclockwise, must be passed over and down through the knot, emerging alongside the stem or standing part of the rope, as the directional arrow indicates. Thus you have *doubled* the *Crown Knot.*

All that remains is to dispose of the strand ends, and there are two ways to do it. They may be cut off close under the knot, or they may be left fairly long, scraped

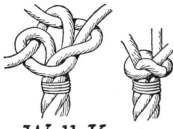

Wall Knot

Crown Knot

Wall-and-
Crown

Manrope Knot

Matthew Walker's
Knot

to a taper and served over, as I have shown. The latter is preferable as there is no possibility of the knot coming apart.

Before some eagle-eyed expert criticizes my technical accuracy I had better draw a few fine distinctions relative to this knot. The true Tack Knot was tied originally in the *tack,* which was a rope used to haul forward the weather clew of a lower square sail, and of course was always tied with 3 strands. The true *Manrope Knot,* however, was always tied with four or five strands, and was used in the *manropes,* at the side ladder or gangway. I don't suppose that the yachtsman with a 30-foot sloop gives a damn one way or another, but I just don't want some chronic finger-pointer taking potshots at me over a point of historical accuracy.

But whether you tie this knot with 3, 4, or more strands and regardless of what you may call it you will find it both handsome and useful. It has the bulk so desirable in a terminal knot, is symmetrical and compact, and most important of all it is easily remembered.

Matthew Walker's Knot

Matthew Walker is reputed to have been the only sailor to have had a knot named for him, and by virtue of this oddity both he and the knot have been revered by countless generations of seamen wherever ships have sailed. Stranger still, no one seems to know for sure just who he was or if he actually existed at all. The first printed reference to Matthew Walker's Knot is found in D'arcy Lever's THE SHEET ANCHOR, published in London in 1808. Many authorities believe that such a man did live, and that he was probably a master-rigger in a British naval dockyard.

True or not, it's a good story and who am I to disturb so ancient and honored a tradition? Most important is the fact that this is the best of all *lanyard* knots. The true lanyard knot is a form of stopper knot tied somewhere within the length of a lanyard; that is to say that the rope strands forming the knot emerge from the top or crown and are then laid up again and whipped. A lanyard knot is tied in the end of a shroud lanyard to prevent its reeving through the deadeye. It is also employed in lanyards of small stuff, such as marlinspike, knife or bosun's whistle lanyards, as well as various decorative gear.

Matthew Walker's Knot may be tied with any number of strands, and a 6-strand knot is of course more handsome than one of 3 strands. Irrespective of the number of strands, all have the same basic structure and all are tied in the same manner. Thus the accompanying illustrations will serve for all, should you desire to try the more complicated forms.

I suggest you practice the knot with a length of ⅜ inch rope. Put a stout seizing of marline about 12 inches from the end, unlay the rope to the seizing and put a stopping of twine on the end of each strand. Take the left hand strand and *wall* it, as shown in the first sketch. You will notice that the strand thus encircles the body of the rope and comes up through its own bight, in effect forming a half-knot. Now wall the next strand, by encircling the rope and passing the strand up through *both* bights, as shown in the second sketch.

Then wall the remaining strand, and this time the strand comes up through all *three* bights. The third sketch shows the sequence of all three strands quite clearly, and if you wish to tie the knot with 4, 5, or 6 strands or more the sequence would be the same, and all you need to remember is that each successive strand must pass through the bight of each preceding strand in proper order.

With the knot now set up, arrange the strands neatly so that they emerge from the center of the knot and one by one draw up the slack, a little at a time, until the knot is well seated close on to the seizing and firm and compact. Now lay the strands up into rope again, to their original lay, and put on a palm-and-needle whipping, and then trim off neatly.

The Turk's Head

There is probably no *decorative* knot of greater usefulness than the Turk's Head, nor has any knot ever been so popular with the sailor. For over three hundred years it has been recognized as the preferred tubular knot for applying to cylindrical objects such as stanchions, rails, and ropes. On the practical side it is used on the top spoke of the steering wheel to mark the "dead-center" position, and at spaced intervals on bowsprit shrouds and footropes it provides a safe foothold. On tool handles it gives a better handgrip, and on the loom of an oar makes an excellent drip guard.

Its purely ornamental uses are too numerous to catalogue. Whenever a handrail or stanchion is served over or given a decorative covering, the Turk's Head marks

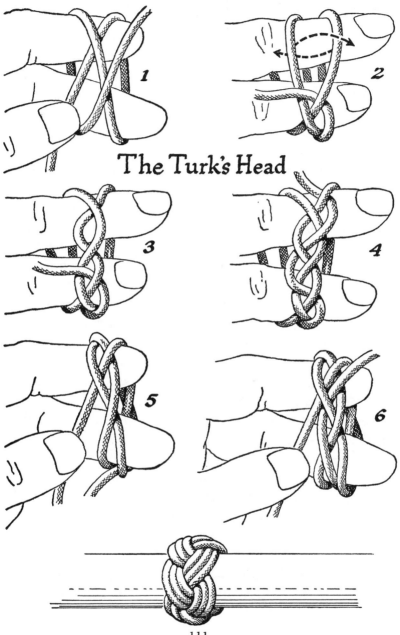

The Turk's Head

the beginning and the end. Sea chest beckets, rope handles of all sorts, bag lanyards and bell pulls all are dressed up in proper style by this handsome, single-strand knot. There are literally hundreds of variations and elaborations of the Turk's Head, many of which require intricate diagrams and countless hours of tedious work to complete.

For the yachtsman it is sufficient to know but one good Turk's Head, simple to tie and easy to remember. The knot I have chosen is the one most universally known and used, and adequate for most every need. It is a 5-bight knot, triple passed, which means that there are 5 scallops or bights around the rim of the knot. It should be noted that Turk's Heads are only tied in small stuff; marline, seine twine, or all forms of light, cotton line. I have found that nothing equals small braided cotton for the purpose, particularly to practice with, since it does not come unlaid or get twisted and kinked.

To learn how to tie this knot it is best to tie it about your fingers, rather than a permanent object, for it is easier to rotate the knot as you progress. Take two turns about the fingers as shown in the first sketch. Rotate the fingers toward you and tuck the working end as shown in the second sketch. Now pass a bight of the right hand turn to the left, under a bight of the left hand turn, as shown in the third sketch.

The working end is now tucked through the bight just formed, from back to front, then across to the right and through the turn just above, as the fourth sketch indicates. Now rotate the fingers away from you and you'll find you are right back at the starting point, as in sketch #5.

The basic knot has now been set up and is ready for doubling, which means passing the working end completely through the circuit of the knot. To double the knot the working end is laid alongside of the opposite end and is then taken all through the knot, following the same over-and-under sequence, and keeping always parallel to and on the same side of the same strand or part. When the starting point is reached again the working end is passed through the knot once more in the same manner, and the knot is now said to be "triple-passed," and complete.

In the actual application of the Turk's Head knot to an object it must be drawn up taut and firm, to grip the object tightly and to prevent its ever loosening. Like all decorative knots it should first be set up loosely for ease in working. With the marlinspike as a lever you lift a strand or part, and proceed through the knot taking up the slack until every part is tight and the knot assumes an even, symmetrical form. The ends are then cut off close underneath, and if the knot has been drawn up tightly enough the resultant friction will hold the ends securely. With the ends so hidden the Turk's Head knot always fascinates the uninitiated, for it seems to have neither beginning nor end.

When used outside, as on stanchions, rails or footropes it is customary to paint all Turk's Heads—white if made of cotton line or black if made of marline. This not only makes it weather proof but securely cements it in place.

XIII

Ornamental Coverings and Nettings

The arts to be described in this chapter are in the main intended to be used for covering various round or cylindrical objects in a decorative manner, both for practical reasons and for appearance. To mention but a few applications, there are handrails and stanchions, tiller handgrips, ringbolts and handles of all kinds, and protective coverings for water jugs and other breakable containers. With the knowledge of these arts at your command you will normally discover many other places where their judicious use is indicated.

Now it is true that a common serving may be applied to a rail or stanchion, but it is too plain and ordinary looking for a yacht. It just doesn't have the character and delicate refinement needed to accompany fine cabinet work, and smacks too much of the work boat or naval craft. The types of coverings I am suggesting here are all beautiful, and are so varied in character and texture that they will be suitable for practically any application.

The material used for these coverings is common seine twine, known variously as netting twine, white line or cod line. It is put up in skeins or hanks and is available in several sizes. Since it is made of cotton it has the abominable habit of unlaying when cut, and with fraying ends it is impossible to work with. A drop of Duco cement on the cut ends prevents unlaying and makes it easy to tuck and manipulate.

Cockscombing

Cockscombing is a form of hitched covering applied to a rail, stanchion or ring. Originally it was a form of chafing gear used primarily to cover ringbolts, and was commonly known as *Ringbolt Hitching*. It consists of a continuous series of half hitches made with from one to six strands or cords, and the character of the resultant design may be varied by altering the direction of the hitches and by different groupings of the strands. If there are ringbolts anywhere on your yacht it is an excellent idea to cover them in this manner, not only because it protects a rope that is rove through them from chafe, but it acts as a fender and keeps the rings from rattling. Hatches, doors and drawers are often fitted with bronze rings as handles and they would be dressed up considerably by Cockscombing.

The first type shown is the common *3-strand Cockscomb,* which has a neat "braid" design. It should be noted that in covering a ring the hitches should be taken so that the design is at the *outer circumference* of the ring. As the sketches indicate, each strand is hitched alternately to the right and left. Draw them up snugly and take care to keep the hitches in perfect alignment.

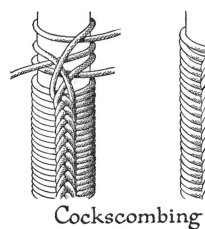

Cockscombing French Hitching

Needle Hitching

Fender Hitching

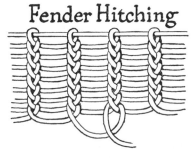

Underhand Grafting Overhand Grafting

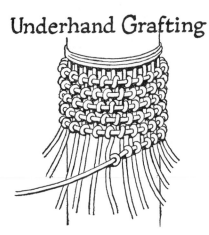

An interesting variation may be had by using three *doubled* strands—it results in a wider design with a little more character.

Next is the *3-strand Running Cockscomb,* in which all three strands are hitched to the right and then reversed and hitched to the left. It may be varied by using 2, 4, or even 5 strands, as your fancy dictates.

French Hitching

This spiral form of hitching is suitable only for covering a handrail or stanchion of considerable length. As the sketch indicates, a single strand is continuously hitched to the right, and the ridge formed by the hitches spirals around the rail in a manner suggestive of the lay of rope. The hitches should be taken tightly and evenly, and the finished work will be greatly enhanced if given several coats of white paint.

Needle Hitching

This is perhaps the commonest and the most versatile of all hitched coverings. It is generally used to cover small objects of almost any shape and as its name implies, is worked with a sail needle. Whalers muffled their oarlocks with needle hitching of marline. Using small-size fishline the sailor of old would cover his knife sheath, his needle case, and the handles of various tools. I have even seen a clay pipe some sailor had covered with fine hitching to protect it from breaking.

The texture of needle hitching is such that it provides a non-slip surface for anything that may be grasped with the hand, even though wet with perspiration or covered with grease. For that reason I have used it to cover screwdriver and icepick handles, and have found it superior to serving for tillers. Applied to the lower half of drinking glasses and varnished, it makes an attractive, removable, and non-skid holder.

Thread a sail needle with a long piece of fishline and take one or two turns with the end about the object to be covered, and then put a series of loose hitches all around. Then start a second round of hitches, but this time put them on the series of loops formed by the first row of hitches, and continue in this manner until the object is covered. If the object tapers omit a hitch at regular intervals, and where it increases in diameter simply add a hitch or two each time around. Obviously, the hitches should be uniform in size and fairly snug.

Fender Hitching

Here we have the perfect covering for a water jug or bottle. For this purpose you should use tarred fishline threaded in a large sail needle. The ribbed effect greatly resembles a knitted sweater, and it acts as a perfect fender—in fact, this form of hitching was formerly used for covering fenders, which accounts for its name.

It is started in the same manner as needle hitching, but all subsequent hitches are taken about the *neck* of the hitches in the preceding row, instead of on the bights. The ribs may be as close together as you desire, depending on the size or length of the loops. For a professional job the ribs must be perfectly aligned and straight. Tapering is achieved as in needle hitching, by omitting or adding hitches.

Underhand Grafting

Despite the sinister implications of its name, this is an entirely legal and ethical form of covering used where a rather smooth texture is desired. Often called Spanish Hitching, Grafting consists of numerous strands of fine fishline, called *fillers*, hitched continuously about a spirally wound line called the *warp*. In the old days block straps were often grafted over to keep out moisture, for the texture of grafting is quite fine, and when painted forms a covering that is practically waterproof. Rope handles and sea chest beckets were also given this form of covering.

In most cruising centerboard yachts it is customary to run the centerboard pennant through a brass tube or pipe extending from the top of the case to the cabin top. Thus it serves in three ways—it hides the pennant, gives structural support to the cabin top and provides a welcome handhold when you are below deck in a seaway. Now instead of polishing that brass pipe over and over, only to see it tarnish over night, it is an excellent idea to give it a decorative covering such as we are discussing. Grafting is perfectly suited for this, with a short section of *Coachwhipping* in the center for variety, and Turk's Heads marking the ends of each section.

The warp, which is approximately 30 times as long as the filler strands, should be of stiffer material than the fillers, and I have found that tarred "cuttyhunk" is excellent for the purpose. A sufficient number of filler strands to cover the stanchion are hitched close together on the end of the warp, which is then seized in position.

The warp is held in the left hand, and as it is wound about the stanchion clockwise, each filler strand is hitched about it in turn with the right hand. The warp must be held taut at all times and the hitches taken snugly.

Overhand Grafting

This is done exactly like the Underhand Grafting except that the hitches are taken *overhand,* or reversed. It is by far a handsomer covering, and the texture resembles snakeskin, or heavy canvas. In my opinion Grafting should always be painted over, with semigloss white. It not only improves the appearance but it makes it easy to keep clean—a little soap and water will then remove the inevitable finger marks.

Coachwhipping

Because of its bold, masculine design this is perhaps the most handsome of all coverings for rail or stanchion. Actually it is a form of round sennit with a core—the core being the rail or stanchion. Generally made with seine twine, it may also be made with braided cotton line up to 1/8 inch in diameter, the greater the diameter of the object to be covered, the heavier the material. It may be worked with 4, 6, or 8 strands, each "strand" being composed of 2 or 3 parallel cords or lines.

4-strand Coachwhipping does not hide the object to be covered completely. 8-strand is so involved that no one but an octopus could handle it alone. I have chosen the 6-strand as being most practical for the average individual, for it is fairly simple, hides well, and

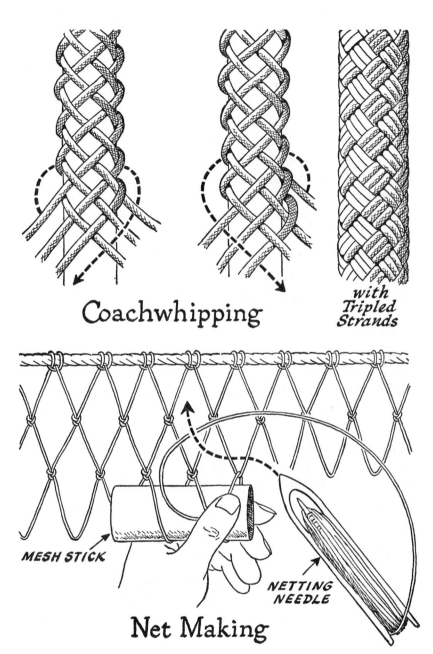

Coachwhipping

with
Tripled
Strands

MESH STICK

NETTING
NEEDLE

Net Making

does not require the services of a helper. For the sake of clarity I have shown 6 *single* strands in the sketches, which I recommend you use for practice purposes. Not until you have mastered the sequence and the technique should you attempt using doubled or tripled strands.

The best way to practice Coachwhipping is to clamp a short length of broom-handle vertically in a vise, and near the top seize 6 lengths of heavy cord, evenly spaced. Now pass the *left rear* strand around the back to the right, then forward under one, over one and under one, and then across to the left side, as shown in the second sketch. Then pass the *right rear* strand across in back to the left and bring it forward under, over, and under the strands, and carry it across in front to the right, as in the third sketch.

Continue by repeating the cycle, alternately passing the left and right rear strands as shown. Warning—don't go away leaving the job unfinished, for it is sometimes very confusing to come back and find you don't know just where you left off or where to start again.

In working with double or triple strands it is difficult to keep them from tangling, and you will find that it helps to wind each set of strands in a small coil and snap a rubber band on. Thus the surplus line is kept under control and is easily withdrawn as needed.

Net Making

Although netting is not properly classed as decorative work, it is a form of hitching, and I feel justified in including it here because many yachtsmen had expressed a desire to learn the method of making it. Some want to make their own crab nets, or a net bag to hold sail stops, and perhaps a "Pullman" net to be slung over a berth to hold clothes or personal gear.

Net making requires the use of two tools—the Netting Needle and the Mesh Stick. The Netting Needle, which holds a supply of seine twine and serves as a shuttle for tying the knots, is easily obtained at most fishing supply stores. The Mesh Stick, which is a gauge for determining the size of the meshes, can be easily made since it is nothing more than a flat stick about 4 inches long, its width depending on the size of the mesh desired.

The Mesh Knot is basically a *Sheet Bend* tied with the netting needle. The first row or tier of meshes are generally tied to the "headline" of a net with a series of evenly spaced Clove Hitches, as shown in the sketch. The second row of meshes is started by tying the mesh knot to each mesh of the first row, holding the mesh stick in the left hand as shown in the second sketch. To taper a net, as for a crabnet, every third or fourth knot is tied through 2 *adjoining meshes,* instead of one.

XIV

Sennit Making

In the days of the sailing ships the ancient art of sennit making was a commonplace chore to the sailor, for sennits of various kinds were a necessary part of the ship's gear, and through normal wear and tear required constant replacement. Robands, sea gaskets, reef beckets, lanyards and all manner of chafing gear were made of some form of sennit.

Today those needs no longer exist, and sennit is useful to the yachtsman only to a limited degree. It is required for making bag lanyards, bell pulls, rope handles and beckets, and since most yachtsmen enjoy making these articles, if only for their decorative value, I shall discuss some of the basic designs that are most useful. The best material for sennit making is braided cotton, flag halyard stuff, or small cotton line.

Plaited Sennits

As the name indicates, these are plaited, braided or woven, and may be flat, round or square. The first sketch shows the familiar 3-strand flat sennit, identical to the little girl's braided pigtails, and requires no explanation. The second sketch shows 4-strand flat sennit,

3-STRAND 4-STRAND
Flat Sennits

4-STRAND
Square Sennit

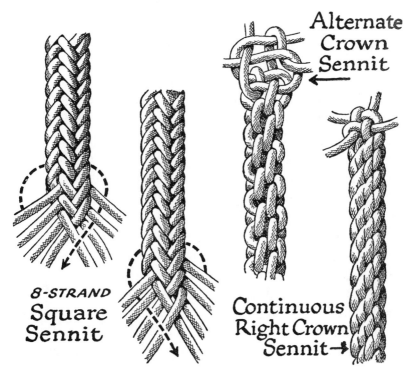

Alternate Crown Sennit

←

8-STRAND
Square Sennit

Continuous Right Crown Sennit →

which has a different sequence. Notice that the outside left hand strand is passed *in front,* over the next strand, and the outside right hand strand is passed *in back,* or *under* the adjacent strand. Flat sennits may be made with as many as 12 strands, but these two are sufficient for the yachtsman.

The next sketch shows 4-strand square sennit. Strangely enough, square sennit may also be round, and vice versa. If you roll square sennit under your foot it will become round and smooth. Hit it with a mallet on all four sides and it will be square. First the upper left strand is passed around in back, then forward between the right hand strands and across to the left side again. Then the right hand top strand is passed around in back, forward between the two left hand strands and across to the right again. Continue by passing alternately the left and right outside strands.

Last is the 8-strand square sennit, the most useful of the two, which is handsome, firm, and non-stretching. Like the 4-strand, it is made in two movements. The strands are divided with 4 strands held in the left hand and 4 in the right. First the top left strand is passed around in back and brought forward between the center of the right hand strands, then carried across to the left, at the bottom. Next the right hand strand is passed in back, then to the front through the center of the left hand group and across to the right bottom.

All sennits should be made tightly and solidly, or the result will be flimsy and limp. Since all square sennits are tubular in section they may be worked about a core and hence may be used to cover a rail or stanchion. If

4 or 8 strand sennit is so used, with *doubled* or *tripled* strands the result will be Coachwhipping.

Crown Sennits

These sennits are firmer and have more body than the plaited type, and have quite a different character. They are made by tying a continuous series of crown knots, one on top of the other. Any number of strands may be used, from 3 to 10, and since these too are tubular they may be made about a core; in fact if more than 6 strands are used a core is a necessity. I have chosen the 4-strand sennit because of its simplicity—all others are made in identically the same manner.

The first shown is *Alternate Crown Sennit,* known in the British Navy as *Nelson Sennit,* in honor of their famous hero. Seize four strands together and tie a right hand crown knot, as shown in the sketch. Next crown the four strands to the *left,* on top of the right crown. Then crown to the right again and continue, *ad infinitum,* alternately crowning to left and right. By using *doubled* strands a different effect is achieved, and a more handsome sennit results.

The *Continuous Right Crown Sennit* has a spiral effect that resembles right-laid rope, and also may be made with double strands. No directions are necessary, for as its name implies it is achieved by tying a continuous series of right crowns, one on top of another.

XV

Chafing Gear

Among the minor perils of the sea are the destructive effects of chafe and friction resulting from the constant working and rubbing together of sails, rigging, spars and gear. The instant a vessel becomes waterborne there begins within her a vital, restless movement that never ceases for a moment throughout her life afloat. All through her hull there is a continual working of timber upon timber, an imperceptible, never-ending movement that no amount of bracing, strapping or shoring can ever still. It is this movement that gives her life and animation and endows her with a personality. Without it she becomes but an inert mass in which there is neither spirit nor pleasure.

The deterioration of a hull from this constant flexing and working is very gradual and noticeable only after years of use. In fact the ability of a given hull to retain its elasticity in spite of the perpetual movement of its parts determines the length of its useful life. But every movement of the hull is transmitted instantly to the spars, rigging and sails, and it is with these that we are immediately concerned, for it is here that the resultant damage from chafe and wear can be immediate and apparent.

In the days of the square-riggers, with their maze of complex rigging and gear, the prevention of chafe was a serious problem. Sails were chafed by the standing rigging, the standing rigging by the spars, and the running rigging by all three. Careful, periodic inspection and the judicious application of chafing gear were, and still are, the only means of combating the damage caused by chafe.

In modern yachts the problem still exists, fortunately to a lesser degree, but while chafing gear is much simpler the prudent skipper still makes careful, periodic inspection, ever alert for the first sign of possible damage.

Sails are particularly susceptible to injury from chafe. Jibs and headsails are generally free and clear of anything liable to cause interference, but mainsails and mizzens bear on the spreaders when the booms are broad off and chafe badly at the point of contact. Topping lifts and lazyjacks are in constant motion when under way, rubbing back and forth on the sails and slowly but inevitably doing their damage.

Chafing gear for the protection of sails is known as *baggy-wrinkle*, a handmade affair of rope yarns which is wound spirally about the offending wire or rope to form a soft, brush-like, cylindrical buffer or fender. Just why it was given such a peculiar name no one seems to know, its origin being lost somewhere in the misty past, but its soft resilience and considerable diameter make it well nigh perfect for the job it is intended to do.

Most yachtsmen accumulate numerous coils of old rope, rope that is "too poor to use and too good to throw away." In the making of baggy-wrinkle you can put it to work, for the first step is to chop some of it up into identical pieces about 5 or 6 inches long. These pieces must then be unlaid or separated into individual yarns until you have a sizable pile of them.

Middle a length of marline 10 or 12 feet long and stretch it up waist high between two convenient points. Upon this doubled marline the yarns, called *thrums* or *rovings,* are to be hitched and jammed close together, the ends hanging down and forming a sort of fringe the length of the marline. Standing near one end with the doubled marline under the right arm, lay a yarn across the under side of the marline, bring the left end up, over and down between the two parts, then pass the right end up, over and down between. Do likewise with a second yarn, and grasping the ends beneath slide it along the marline and jam it up against the first yarn.

Continue in a like manner until the marline is completely filled. The operation is very simple, as the illustration clearly shows. Only the yarns from manila rope should be used, for no other fiber has the necessary wiriness.

To apply the baggy-wrinkle at the spreaders, one end is seized to the shroud about 6 or 8 inches below the spreader tip and it is then wound closely about the wire, past the spreader and for an equal distance above where it is finished off with another seizing.

Thus you have accomplished two things—you have protected the sail from the chafe and wear, and elimi-

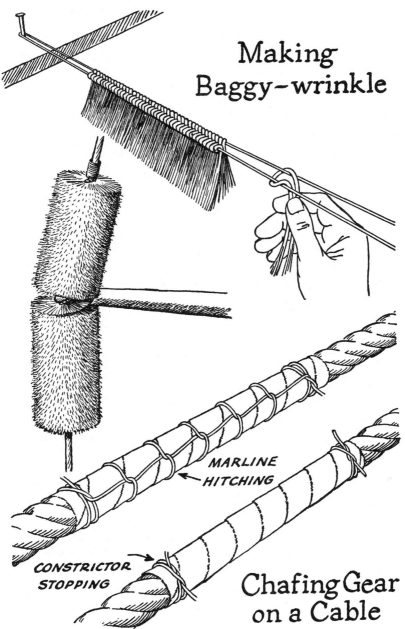

Making
Baggy-wrinkle

MARLINE
HITCHING

CONSTRICTOR
STOPPING

Chafing Gear
on a Cable

131

nated the tendency of the sail to foul on the spreader tips, and both of these objectives deserve a little explanation.

In the first place, most sails are machine sewn, and this means that the stitches lie on the surface of the cloth for it is impossible to get enough tension on the thread to sink it in properly. Hand sewn sails are stronger and have a longer life because the stitches are below the surface and not exposed to wear. Thus it will be seen that when a rope or wire continually rubs against a machine sewn sail it is the stitching and not the cloth that suffers, and when the sail approaches old age it generally lets go at the seams first. The bulk or diameter of baggy-wrinkle keeps the sail away from the wire and its softness prevents the chafe.

The interference of spreaders is peculiar only to mainsails that are jib-headed. When running off before a strong wind part of the sail presses hard against the lee spreader, while the balance, or the part extended by the battens, falls around behind or to leeward of the spreader. Generally a deep wrinkle or fold is formed at the spreader tip on a line with the inner ends of the battens. Now if the boat should be jibed accidentally, or if you fail to trim the sheet in before executing a jibe, invariably the inner end of a batten will catch on the shroud and a torn sail, broken spreader or both will result. Baggy-wrinkle properly applied greatly lessens the danger of the sail becoming fouled in this manner.

The chafing of topping lifts and lazyjacks is more prevalent in gaff-rigged yachts than those with the jib-headed rig. Here again the judicious application of baggy-wrinkle prevents the slow but steady wearing away of the stitching. Often a section barely 6 inches long placed at the point of maximum chafe will suffice. In a larger yacht with a more complex rig you might need several at spaced intervals—your own common sense dictates the size of the dose.

With the wide diversity in size and rig of yachts it is impossible to designate specifically each and every point where chafe may occur—the most that can be said is that chafe is where you find it. Nevertheless there is one point where chafe occurs in every vessel that floats, and that is the chock through which an anchor rode or mooring line is led.

A rope cable is elastic and resilient, and as the yacht surges on it to each passing wave it alternately stretches and recovers. This inherent resilience cushions the shock of each blow and eases the strain, and the widespread popularity of Nylon anchor cable is due to its possessing this characteristic to a far greater degree than any other fiber.

But as the cable stretches and recovers it saws back and forth in the chock unceasingly *under great tension.* Here we have chafe that is really serious. To the uninitiated the beautifully polished surface of a chromium-plated chock might seem incapable of doing serious damage to a husky rope, but I have seen a 1-inch brand-new cable that was chafed half way through in less than an hour while a 40 foot yacht lay at anchor during a blow, all because her owner was too lazy or indifferent to apply chafing gear. Only the amazing strength of its Nylon fibers kept that cable from parting.

Wherever a cable or mooring line passes through a chock, or across a rail, chafing gear should be applied, not only to protect such lines from injury, but to guard against the yacht's going adrift as a result of their chafing through and parting. The only alternative is to stand by constantly to haul in or pay out the cable a few inches at frequent intervals to bring the point of chafe to another spot. This operation is called "freshening the nip" and seems rather silly when chafing gear can be clapped on in a minute or two.

The preferred way is to parcel the cable with a bit of old canvas seized in position with marline. I carry a number of strips of canvas about 3 inches wide in my ditty box at all times just for this purpose. The strip of canvas is wound spirally about the rope *against* the lay for a distance of not less than 18 inches. Most authorities recommend that it then be *"marled over,"* which is to seize the parcelling with a series of *marline hitches* as I have illustrated. However, I prefer just a single stopping with a *constrictor knot* at each end. The marline hitches quickly chafe through and come adrift, but nothing will ever cause a constrictor knot to let go. In wrapping the canvas strip around the rope be sure to overlap it for at least half its width. Thus the rope is protected by two layers of canvas.

If a yacht is regularly berthed alongside a bulkhead or dock the mooring lines should be treated in a like manner. But since they customarily have a spliced loop for securing to post or bollard the loop itself should likewise be parcelled about its entire circumference;

otherwise the loop becomes badly chafed long before the line itself is worn out.

In recent years sheepskin has had considerable popularity as chafing gear, particularly in small craft, and I suspect it is because it is less unsightly than baggy-wrinkle. It is cut into strips and wrapped around the wire in the same manner. I have used it successfully to cover the bullet-blocks of my lazyjacks, and the soft, compact nature of the wool makes it excellent for points where the chafe is relatively minor. However it is unsatisfactory for spreaders since it lacks the bulk of baggy-wrinkle and so fails to keep the sail off the wire and the spreader ends.

Chafing gear is often applied to spars. In the days of the square-riggers this was in the form of mats or sennit, hand woven aboard the ship and lashed in place. In the modern small yacht I know of but two places where it is required. First, when running dead before the wind it is often desirable to carry the boom as far forward as it will go. Thus the boom saws up and down on the shroud and chafes severely. The best treatment here is to tack a strip of rawhide or leather on either side of the boom at the point of contact.

In the second instance, where an overlapping jib is carried the sheet blocks and clew cringle flog the mast every time you go about, and the mast soon becomes badly scarred and unsightly. Here again a square of hide neatly tacked around the mast gives ample protection.

There is often considerable chafe encountered in

running rigging, but in this instance chafing gear is not the answer. Invariably it is the result of improper lead of sheets or halyards or bad positioning of blocks and fairleads and can be corrected by their rearrangement. Generally speaking chafing gear is resorted to only where chafe is *unavoidable*.

XVI

The Technique of Reefing

Every year a new crop of enthusiasts are introduced to yachting through the medium of small-boat racing. Yacht clubs today give every encouragement to the beginner, particularly the youngsters, and offer competent instructors in sailing and racing, to the end that they may take their rightful places in the highly-developed modern racing classes. But since the ultimate goal is racing a Snipe, Lightning, Star or whatever one-design class is currently popular around that particular club, the instructor's field of interest is often slightly restricted and his teaching is confined to the needs of those classes. This results in the student's range of knowledge being rather narrow, and in one particular very inadequate.

It would seem that a whole generation is being brought up with the belief that reefing is ruinous to sails and is entirely unnecessary. A surprising number of otherwise experienced yachtsmen have never turned in a reef and have but a vague idea as to how it is done, and all because their entire sailing experience has been acquired in class boats which *never* reef. In some respects I suppose it has an element of humor, but in my opinion it is a downright serious condition and that is why I am devoting this chapter to the art of reefing, in an attempt to dispel some of those false beliefs.

Reefing does *not* ruin a sail. A well made sail, if reefed correctly and properly handled, will not be harmed nor will its usefulness be impaired in any respect. Many sails *have* been ruined, torn or overstretched by improper reefing—it's all in knowing how to do it—and, what's equally important, understanding the reasons for doing it in that particular and correct manner.

When the sailmaker provides for a reef in constructing a sail he knows precisely where the strains will come and how to obtain the strength required to resist those strains. A reefed sail is secured to the boom at the same points and in much the same manner as the full sail—at the leech and luff, and at spaced intervals across the body of the sail. The reef points, or the holes for a lacing line are spaced the same distance apart as the slides on the roped foot of the sail. Thus the reefed sail has the same support as the full sail, with one exception—there is no roping across the line of the reef.

Now if you were to spread your sail out smoothly and sight along the reef band (or line of reef points) you would discover that the reef cringles at the luff and leech are an inch or so *above* the line, the amount varying with the size of the sail. I daresay that not one yachtsman in fifty has ever noticed this, or understands why the sailmaker placed the cringles out of line. Most of the strain along the foot of the sail is an upward pull, and the roping supports the sail uniformly throughout its length, tying the points of attachment—the sail slides —together.

Since roping the sail across the line of reef points is hardly practical, the sailmaker does the next best thing —he places the reef cringles above the line so that they take some of the strain off the foot of the sail. Thus the reefed sail can assume a normal shape with the reef points under no greater tension than the sail slides would have in the unreefed sail.

The best way to learn to reef correctly is to pick a day when there is little or no wind and practice the operation at your mooring. Then you can take your time, study each step and observe the results, without the sail flogging about in the breeze and fighting you all the way.

The first important point to remember is that you should *never* hoist or lower the sail with the boom unsupported. When the partially hoisted sail is forced to carry the weight of the boom a terrific strain is set up diagonally across the sail from the clew to the luff, and the sail is stretched out of shape. The best way to prevent this from happening is to see that your yacht is rigged with a topping-lift and to *use it*. In its simplest form the topping-lift runs from the masthead to the boom-end, then through a hole in the boom or through a cheek-block, and is belayed to a small cleat on the side of the boom. *Before* hoisting or lowering sail the topping-lift should be set up sufficiently to raise the boom above its normal position; then the sail may be raised or lowered without bearing a strain other than its own weight.

With the boom supported by the topping-lift or boom crutch the *first step* in reefing is to lash the reef cringle in the luff to the tack cringle with a short length of light line. Explicit directions cannot be given for the *manner* of lashing because not all gooseneck or boom fittings are alike. But this much is certain, the reef cringle *must* be positioned *exactly opposite* or *alongside of* the tack cringle. Pass the lashing through both cringles as many times as the space will permit, because it must be secure, and finish off the ends with a slipped reef-knot.

The *second step* is to secure the reef cringle in the leech to the boom with another lashing. Two things must be accomplished here—the reef cringle must be hauled *out,* just as the clew was when the sail was bent, and held *down* to the boom by a lashing, just as the outhaul fitting holds down the clew. The simplest way of doing this is to secure a light but strong line to the reef cringle with a bowline knot, and reeve the end through a hole in the end of the boom, unless a block has already been provided for the purpose. Then the end is rove through the cringle once more and again through the boom-end. Thus you have a *purchase* with which the cringle can be hauled out.

Now lay out the sail fairly along the boom with the reef points aligned, and haul out the leech of the sail *firmly.* To hold all you have gained pass the end of the line through the cringle and take a half-hitch about the standing part close to the cringle. If a slipped half-hitch is used, the loop can be secured under the turns of the line for security. When shaking out the reef, the slipped half-hitch can easily be undone, whereas a plain half-hitch can be difficult. Now take several turns around the boom, *through the cringle,* bearing in mind that the cringle must be held in a *vertical* position, exactly *the same height above the boom as the clew cringle.* Then secure the lashing with a couple of half-hitches.

You are now ready for the *third step,* the tying in of the reef points. First pull out the surplus canvas from between the reef band and the boom, so it hangs down fairly throughout its length, on the *starboard side.* Furl, or roll it neatly, and starting at the center of the boom, start tying the reef points. Pass the reef nettle on the port side between the roping and the boom and bring it up over the furled sail to its starboard mate and tie a Slipped Reef Knot. Do *not* try to see how tightly you can tie it, or you will strain and injure the cloth—just be sure the sail is rolled and tied firmly. Now tie the rest of the points, working both ways from the center, being careful to get the same tension at each point.

Hoist your sail fully now, slack off on the topping lift, and take a look at your first attempt. Here is what to look for in the way of mistakes. If there are a number of short, hard wrinkles fanning out from each reef point, and the cloth looks hard, taut, and flat between, you have tied the reef points down too tightly, or the luff and leech cringles are set too high. If only one or two of the reef points have this characteristic, they should be slacked off a bit. If the reef has been turned in correctly there should be a slight fullness all along the foot of the sail.

If several long, hard wrinkles fan out upward from

the cringle at the leech, and there is a slackness in the leech in the first foot or more above the boom, it generally indicates that you have hauled out the sail too far. There are bound to be some wrinkles at the leech, but they should be soft and few in number. If you have not hauled the sail out enough it will be indicated by wrinkles fanning out from each reef point, *plus* a fullness between the points.

It is difficult to learn how to judge the turning in of a reef from a written description, because there is no substitute for experience. Therefore it is an excellent idea to have an experienced person along when you attempt your first reef, for his constructive criticism can quickly reveal the worth of your efforts, and give you confidence.

Having covered the fundamentals of reefing technique, there remains the equally important operation of shaking out a reef. Here too you should know the how and the why of the procedure. More often than not the reef is taken out while under way, for when the wind moderates to the point where full sail can be carried there is no point to sailing reefed.

It is not necessary to lower the sail entirely to cast off the reef. Haul in the main sheet so the boom is over the quarter and set up the topping-lift. Then lower the sail a foot or so to get some slack in the sail, and if the helmsman luffs a bit it will make the job easier. Now the *first* thing you do is to cast off the reef points to free the bunt of the sail. The second thing is to cast off the lashing of the leech, and *lastly* free the cringle at the luff. This sequence is vitally important. If you were to cast off the cringle lashings first, all of the strain would come on the reef points, and the sail would either be torn or hopelessly stretched out of shape.

With everything cast off the sail can be fully hoisted, the topping-lift slacked off and you are on your way. If you have done a proper job throughout, your sail will set just as it did before you reefed, neither ruined, stretched or harmed in any way.

Many sails, particularly racing sails, do not have reef points. In their place a *lacing line* is used. This is a long single cotton line of suitable diameter which is laced spirally around the rolled up sail, from luff to leech, around the foot and through the holes or grommets in order. The ends of the line are hitched to the luff and leech cringles.

When passing the lace line do not make a hitch at every turn—just a simple spiral will do. This distributes the strain on the sail and allows the foot to assume a more natural shape. Having passed the line and secured the ends, it is necessary to go back and take up the slack, starting at the center and working both ways. The object is to get an even tension all along the reef.

It takes considerably longer to turn in a reef with a lace line than with reef points, but in one respect it would appear to be easier on the sail. Since the lace line is free to slide through the reefing grommets at will, there is no danger of there being a hard spot at any one point—the strain on the cloth is evened up. However, the majority of yachtsmen consider the lace line somewhat of a nuisance, and most sails have reef points.

XVII

Towing Procedures

Every yachtsman can reasonably expect that some day he will be called upon to go to the aid of a fellow mariner in distress. Whether it be a motorboat with a disabled motor, a capsized sailboat with three kids clinging to it or a grounded yacht unable to free herself, it is his bounden duty to give what assistance he can, knowing full well that but for the Grace of God it could well be himself who was in distress. Having been on both ends of a towline I know that such rescue work demands real seamanship if it is to be successful, and that the lack of it can cause more damage than the distressed craft initially suffered. Many a capsized racing skipper has waved off a would-be rescuer, rather than see his boat manhandled by a person he knew to be a poor seaman.

I propose we have a look at the problems involved and the procedures to be followed, so that you may be prepared to give aid in an intelligent manner and are properly equipped for the emergency. Naturally no two incidents are ever alike, nor are the conditions of tide, wind and sea always favorable, but there are enough basic facts involved to enable you to work out a course of action whatever the situation.

Except in the case of the capsized sailboat where the immediate task is fishing the crew out of the water, there is but rarely any great urgency, despite the natural anxiety of those on the distressed boat. Basically, it is generally a towing job, a problem of getting the disabled craft to a place of safety, and it cannot be hurried. Undue haste can only result in damage to one or both of the boats involved.

Because of the many complications involved we'll consider the capsized sailboat first. Upon first sighting the boat there are several things to be done immediately. If your boat is an auxiliary, start the motor and lower all headsails. If it is a sailboat without power, see that your anchor is made up and ready for use. Get several life preservers out on deck, and break out your heaving line and a towline. There is generally ample time to do these things while you are approaching.

I consider a heaving line an absolute necessity. In the first place, in anything but a flat calm it is too dangerous to approach close enough to throw a coil of rope without fouling or falling short. The weighted Monkey's Fist of the heaving line carries the end *in advance of the coil,* and the line travels in a straight arc over and across the distressed boat, as a proper lifeline should. Its lightness enables you to throw it a considerable distance, yet it is strong enough to haul a man through the water to your boat.

You can assume that the other fellow does not have

a suitable towline, and from my experience he rarely does. Every well found yacht should have a spare coil of good Manila stout enough and long enough for towing. Sixty or 70 feet of ⅝ or ¾ inch Manila is a good average size, in my opinion. The heaving line should be bent to the towline with a *Double Sheet Bend* or a *Rolling Hitch*. I prefer the latter if the towline is heavy or stiff, for it is more secure.

Always approach a capsized boat on the windward side, not only to make a lee for her, but to prevent fouling. On the leeward side her mast, sails, and rigging that has gone adrift prevent a safe approach, and her leeward drift is hard to judge. On approaching her a quick glance will reveal the condition of the crew— whether they are exhausted, scared, or in good shape and able to cope with the situation. Your first consideration is the crew, then the salvaging of the boat's sails and gear, and finally the towing job.

With her sails unbent, boom unshipped and running rigging stripped, the average centerboarder can generally be righted without too much difficulty, but to keep her right side up while towing is quite another matter. Filled with water and floating awash she has no stability whatsoever, and only by one or more persons hanging to her rails on either side of the transom can she be kept upright for any length of time.

A swamped boat lies dead in the water and can be moved only with difficulty, therefore the strain imposed in towing is very great. *Never* trust the mooring cleat to hold the towline. Time after time I have seen cleats ripped loose in towing, and occasionally the whole forward deck goes too. The towline should be belayed to the mast at the deck with a *Bowline,* which is not only secure but can be easily untied. Ahead of the Bowline you can take a single round turn about the cleat under the horns, to bring the lead or point of attachment as far forward as possible. Thus the mast takes the strain while the cleat merely snubs the rope.

The best plan is to anchor directly to windward of the boat while preparing for towing. If your boat is a power boat with a wide, high transom, hang a couple of life preservers over the stern and bring the bow of the righted boat close up to bear on them. If the transom of your boat will not permit this, haul the boat up as close as you safely can. If the righted boat is towed too far astern there is danger of her diving under, with disastrous results. Belay the towline to your stern cleat or quarter bitt, but *under no circumstance* make fast. Station a man there holding the towline, with only a couple of turns on the cleat or bitt, so that he may snub the line and ease it out smoothly, or cast off quickly as needed. A crew member must be aboard the towed boat at the stern to keep her righted, if possible, and insist that he secure a lifeline about his waist.

In my estimation a better way to tow the swamped boat is to bring it alongside and lash it fast. Rig all your fenders and a life preserver or two over the side, bring up the boat and secure with both a bow and a stern line. Then make a line fast to the mast with a Clove Hitch, as high as possible, carry it across over the top of your cabin and belay it on the other side. Thus the boat can't capsize away from you, and a man stationed on the side deck can hold the mast off if she comes his way.

When under way with a man in the stern, a boat will very often rise at the bow and free herself of just enough water to enable him to bail furiously with a bucket and eventually empty her. But you can't count on it, and it's enough to get her safely in without damage to either boat.

Above all else tow SLOWLY. Most of the damage in towing is the result of too much power and speed. Tow in a straight course and never broadside to the sea if it can possibly be avoided. If you are towing the boat astern, it is often possible to rig a bridle for better control. Two lines are belayed aft, then brought forward on each side, *outside* the shrouds, and thence to the quarters of your own boat, with a man tending each line.

Where the crew of the capsized boat are too young or inexperienced to be trusted with the task of righting the boat and keeping it under control, your only recourse is to tow the boat as she lays, on her side. All of her gear that can possibly be removed should be taken off before attempting the tow. The towline is belayed to the mast as previously described, but where the line passes the stemhead it must be lashed to the stemhead fitting, for the lead should be as far forward as possible.

The boat should be towed a good boat's length astern —far enough back to prevent her riding up on you, and close enough to see what is happening to her. Your speed should be as slow as you can make it. Your boat will yaw considerably, barely respond to her helm, and will alternately surge on the towline and then slacken off as her stern lifts to every wave. Here is where the man tending the towline can really do his stuff. With but one or two turns about the cleat or bitt he must slack off and snub the line to cushion the shock of every sharp jerk, and haul in when the line goes slack as the towed boat tries to over-ride it. It's something like playing a heavy fish on light tackle.

The main idea is to keep a steady, safe strain on the towline and *never* allow it to fetch up with a violent jerk, for the dead weight of the submerged boat cannot respond to the forward momentum of the tow boat and something has to give—generally your cleat. Unless the tow boat has twin screws, it will gradually wander off her desired course, since the speed through the water is too slow for the rudder to function properly. Periodically the man tending the towline should cast the turns off the cleat or bitt and pay out the line while the skipper revs up his motor to straighten her out and put her back on course.

All attempts at towing the capsized boat should be abandoned if heavy seas are running, for the risk of serious damage and personal injury is very great, particularly for the boat doing the towing. If conditions permit, the distressed boat should be anchored and her position noted by a couple of bearings, then the salvage work can be deferred until the weather moderates.

In towing a disabled power boat or hauling off a boat that has gone aground the procedures are fairly simple, but nevertheless it is important to know the difference between the proper methods and those that can get you into trouble.

Here is the time when you want a *long* towline, and the longer the better. And here is an appropriate time and place to relate an incident and point a moral. It **is** an exhibition of deplorable seamanship that may be seen countless times on whatever waters you sail, year after year. While the scenes may change, the cast of characters and the performance are always the same—right down to the last horrible detail.

A disabled boat is approached by a nearby motorboat manned by an eager johnny-come-lately with an offer to tow. Simultaneously each skipper makes the amazing discovery that this calls for a towline, only they don't think of it as a towline—each in his own mind pictures a vaguely familiar object known as "A Rope." In perfect unison each comes up with a nondescript piece of cordage of doubtful history, and neither piece is long enough to reach from the doghouse to the fence. Without a moment's hesitation one of the skippers remembers his training as a Boy Scout, and with studied carelessness he ties the two "ropes" together with the famous Square Knot. Each skipper now takes his place at the helm and Act II is about to start.

The towboat skipper—the one with the new yachting cap—now guns his motor with a roar to let the other fellow know he has lots of power, drops in the clutch and lurches ahead. Often both ropes are not the same diameter, then "b-o-i-n-n-g!" The Square Knot has come un-squared as the line tautens with a jerk.

If the ropes are the same diameter the Square Knot

will hold and the tow proceeds apace. The climax comes in the final moments of Act III when they reach port. Here they find that it is physically impossible to untie the Square Knot, since the combination of heavy strain and soaking in the water has practically welded the two ropes together. Neither skipper is willing to part with his two-bit half of the towline, so the curtain comes down to "Hearts and Flowers" with one of them doggedly sawing away with a dull, rusty knife.

Now I am not trying to be dramatic, funny or clever, but I have witnessed this performance more times than I can remember, twice with very serious consequences, and I take it as positive proof that missionaries are still needed to bring light to the heathen. For one thing, it demonstrates what I have always preached, that the Square Knot used improperly is the most dangerous knot known. It is a package knot pure and simple, and its only permissible use on a boat is for lashings. The only safe way to unite two ropes is with a *Bend* or a *Splice,* which should be hand tightened carefully.

The reason for using a long towrope is quite obvious. Its sheer weight plus its ability to stretch and recover under a strain causes it to act like a spring, and the shock of a sudden jerk cannot be transmitted from one boat to the other, thus there is less danger of tearing loose a cleat or other fixture. In the case of the grounded boat the spring-like action of a long line actually enables you to exert a greater initial pull than is possible with a short one.

As stated before, if there is the slightest doubt of a

cleat withstanding the strain the towline should be belayed to some strong part of the boat's structure—as near the end of the boat you are towing from as possible. That's the beautiful thing about bitts—they are an integral part of the vessel's structure, securely anchored.

One last important point—the entire coil of the towline should be taken aboard the boat that is doing the towing. Don't let anyone on the distressed boat pass you the end of the line—take the whole coil. Since you are the one with the mobile unit you are the one to have control, and you are the one who will have the fouled propeller if you do otherwise. Station a man at the towline as previously mentioned, and remember the cardinal rule for towing—*take it easy*. Haste makes work for the boys in the boatyards!

XVIII

Some Notes on Cleats and Belaying Pins

Belaying a rope to cleat or pin is such a simple matter that few give it a second thought—take a couple of turns and that's that. So long as it holds without slipping nothing more is required, and why worry about it?

In my humble opinion that's a very unseamanlike attitude to take, even though it's a common one, and probably excusable. There's a lot more to belaying then one might suppose, and since the prudent sailor takes his work seriously I propose we look into it in some detail.

As I see it, two factors are involved in belaying properly—security, which means not only holding without slipping, but the ability to cast off or snub a line with safety, and the prevention of damage to the rope itself. The first is generally a matter of common concern to most yachtsmen, but few give any thought to the constant wear and tear that a rope is subjected to by improper belaying. It all adds up to (1), learning the proper way to belay, (2) having the proper fitting to

153

belay to, and (3) making certain that the fitting is properly installed.

To belay to a cleat or belaying pin is to take a number of S-turns about it—right-hand turns being natural to a right-handed sailor. After enough turns have been taken you *make fast* by taking a single hitch about the horn of the cleat or the handle of the belaying pin. In the case of sheets, a *slipped hitch* is preferable to the single hitch because it can be cast off more quickly, by a quick pull on the sheet end. Since belaying pins are used only for halyards, which are cast off only infrequently, the slipped hitch is not required and is rarely used.

All cleats, with the possible exception of mooring cleats, should be installed at an angle of about 10 degrees to the lead of the sheets or halyards belayed to them. If installed directly in line, as they too frequently are, the round turns are jammed between the standing part and the cleat, it is next to impossible to use the cleat for snubbing, and rapid destruction of the rope by chafe and friction occurs. Since most of the wear in sheets and halyards occurs where they are belayed, it pays to give some thought to the placing of the cleats.

After many years of observation and experience I am convinced that wooden cleats are superior to metal ones in many respects. In the first instance, they are kindlier to rope. Wood, being softer, offers less friction to rope than metal, no matter how well it is polished. Many times I've noticed the telltale bunch of fibers at the base of a bronze mainsheet cleat that revealed the destructive effects of friction. Often I've damned the rope manufacturer for the short life of a jib sheet, when all the time it was the fault of the cleat and not the rope. Since my conversion to wooden cleats the usable life of the sheets has been extended to a surprising degree.

Now to be truthful, much of this wear is due not so much to the fact that the cleat is metal, but to its design and size. I have before me the catalog of one of the foremost manufacturers of yacht hardware, in which are listed the specifications of numerous types of cleats. I notice that in every instance, regardless of the design, a 5-inch cleat is recommended for use with $\frac{3}{8}$ inch rope. Now I am not a design engineer, but from years of practical experience I know very well that a 5-inch cleat can wear out a $\frac{3}{8}$ inch jib sheet in one season. There just isn't enough surface area in a metal cleat that size to give adequate protection from damage by friction. The radius of the curved surface is too small and the rope is sharply bent and distorted beyond a safe factor. The greater the surface area and the easier the curve of the section the less damage will be done to the rope. I use an 8-inch wooden cleat for a $\frac{3}{8}$ inch rope, and my jib sheet will last 3 years.

A common fault of many metal cleats is that they are bored for fastenings too small to hold securely, and all too frequently they are fastened with wood screws. The proper way to secure a cleat to deck or cabin top is to through bolt it, with oak blocking underneath, and the bolts should be on the husky side or the cleat will very soon start working. Screws should never be used, except where the cleat is fastened to a spar, for there is a constant danger of the cleat tearing loose, and if it should, part of the decking is apt to come with it.

In the accompanying drawings I have shown some typical wooden cleats with dimensions for the appropriate proportions. Having used them for many years I know that they are very easy on the rope. Clear, well-seasoned locust is the ideal wood to use, with white oak as a second choice. After roughing out the blanks, they may be finished with a wood rasp and a rat-tail file. It is my practice to soak the cleats in hot linseed oil to prevent checking. After drying for 4 or 5 days they may be varnished or painted, as you prefer.

The first cleat shown is the 8-inch one referred to above, and is suitable for $3/8$ or $1/2$ inch rope. For anything over $1/2$ inch the dimensions should be proportionately increased. The fastenings should be $1/4$ inch carriage bolts, and the holes should be bored with a drill press, for accuracy. It is important that the cleat be finished with care—there should be no sharp curves anywhere and the smoother the cleat the less friction there will be on the rope. Since the cleat is often used for snubbing, the base should be carefully rounded at both ends, for it is here that the greatest friction occurs.

The next cleat shown is a toe jam cleat, which does double duty as a deck block or fairleader. The sheet is led around the wide after end or toe and is belayed by pulling the hauling part sharply across under the long horn, the jamming effect being sufficient to hold the sheet. Crossing turns are not necessary. The cleat must be at an angle with the lead. The principle advantage of a jam cleat is the speed with which the sheet may be

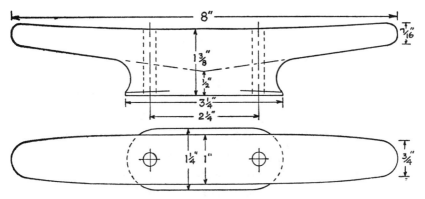

Typical Wood Cleat

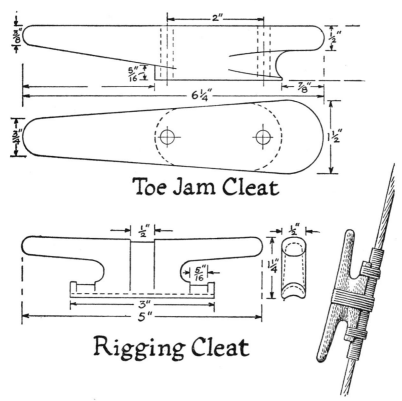

Toe Jam Cleat

Rigging Cleat

belayed or cast off, a quick jerk being sufficient to re-
lease it. Jam cleats are particularly popular with the
racing classes for this reason. It should be noted however that they are hard on the sheets, for in belaying, the
fibers of the rope are severely crushed and rapidly
abraded. I still stick to my original thesis, though, that
regardless of the *type* of cleat a wooden one is much easier on the rope than its metal counterpart.

Next I have shown a rigging cleat for belaying flag
halyards. Because of its small size it should be made
with particular care, and the wood used should be carefully selected for close grain. If you can obtain it,
lignum vitae is ideal. The cleat should be mounted on
the after side of a shroud, breast high, with three stout
seizings of marline and is varnished after it is in place.
The shroud should be parcelled and served for a distance of about 6 inches where the cleat is to be placed.
The grooves for the seizings are made with a file, and the
base is hollowed to fit the served shroud snugly.

XIX

The Boatswain's Chair

One of the most useful articles of ship's furniture is the *Boatswain's Chair,* and certainly no yacht can be called well-found without one. In masted vessels there is frequent need for going aloft, not only for maintenance work but in the periodic inspection of spars, rigging and fittings that is habitual with the prudent skipper. Without this home-made rigger's aid ready at hand it means a trip back to the boatyard and its attendant delays. The obvious alternative is to make one of your own and be able to go aloft at will.

I know of no better way to gain proficiency in the arts of the sailor than in the making of various articles of ship's gear. It adds to your experience, produces something useful and flatters your ego, for it is human nature to take immeasurable pride in things you have made yourself.

Although the making of a proper *boatswain's chair* is an easy task it should be done with extreme care, for if it slips or gives way while you are aloft it can scare hell out of you! The seat should be carefully selected, straight-grained spruce or white cedar not less than 1 inch thick, approximately 10 inches by 22 inches. This is only the *average* size, and you can allow more or less according to your build. Some men have no more hips than an eel, while others are as broad of transom as a Cape Cod catboat.

The bridle or strap should be made of ⅜ or ½ inch *new* Manila, and you will need about 14 feet of it. Bore four holes the size of the rope used, at each of the corners of the seat, keeping sufficiently inboard from the edge to avoid the danger of splitting. Put a temporary whipping on each end of the rope. Now put one end down through one of the holes and pull a couple of feet through. Then reeve the other end down through the hole on the *same side* at the other end of the seat, take it diagonally across the bottom and up through the hole, thence to the other end and down through the remaining hole.

After adjusting the rope so the bridle is the proper length the ends are *short-spliced* together underneath the seat. Now arrange the two bights of the bridle so that they are exactly even and square with the seat and seize them together to form a *double-eyed becket* about 2 inches long. The seizing should be made with marline, with two sets of crossing turns, and must be as tight as possible. Likewise, a round seizing should be put on the two bights where they cross under the seat.

This is the traditional, authentic way to make a professional rigger's chair, and it is completely safe. Even if the seat were to split or break you would still be seated securely in a rope sling.

But it is one thing to own a bo's'n's chair and quite another to know how to use it. First is the problem of

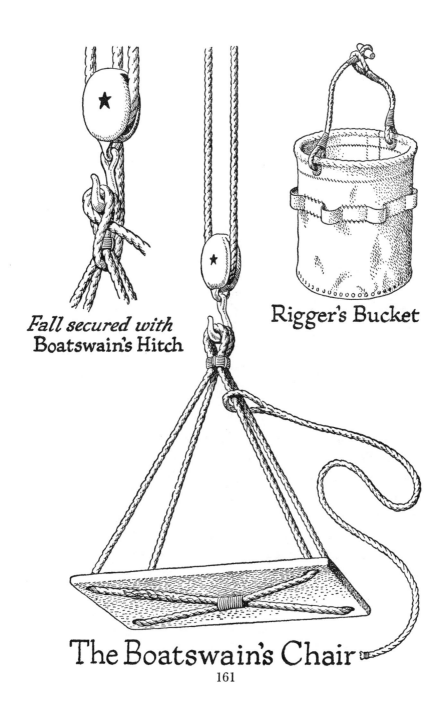

Fall secured with
Boatswain's Hitch

Rigger's Bucket

The Boatswain's Chair

who is going to do the hoisting and how. Then there's the question of keeping one's self from swinging around wildly like a ham on a meat hook once you're aloft. And lastly how to dispose of the miscellaneous assortment of tools required for the particular job, for you can't carry a quart of varnish in the hip pocket of your dungarees.

After many hair-raising experiences being hoisted aloft by well-meaning "helpers" who always got tired at the wrong time, I decided I would much rather do the job myself, single-handed. I can grow old fast enough without any outside help.

Aboard the *Morning Star* I carry at all times a *handy-billy*, also known as a *watch tackle* or *luff tackle*. This is a tackle consisting of a single and a double block, each fitted with a hook, and a ⅜ inch Manila fall long enough to give a usable tackle limit of 35 feet—which is slightly more than the height of my main masthead from the deck.

Now, when I want to go aloft I lay out the tackle along the deck, hook the upper, double block into the headboard shackle of the main halyard, *mouse* the hook with a bit of marline, and hoist the tackle to the masthead with the halyard, which is then belayed and made fast securely to the pin-rail at the foot of the mast. Then I hook the lower block into the becket of the boatswain's chair, with the bill of the hook pointing *towards* me, and I am ready to hoist away.

Since the *luff tackle* has the power of three, it takes but a little over a 50 pound pull to raise my 150 pound carcass aloft. For a much heavier man a *double pur-*

chase could be used instead of the *luff tackle,* for it is comprised of two double blocks and gives the power of four—thus a 50 pound pull lifts 200 pounds.

With this rig you can stop whenever you wish, for a rest or to work, very simply and safely. Just hold the fall with your left hand, and with your right reach through the bridle and pull a bight of the fall forward, then with a half turn of the wrist put a *single hitch* over the bill of the hook. This is known as the *Boatswain's Hitch,* previously described in Chapter V. It is entirely safe and secure, and you now have both hands free for whatever you wish to do, without having to depend on a willing but often inept helper.

It is a wise precaution to rig a lifeline on the chair. A 4 foot length of ⅜ inch Manila or cotton rope is eye-spliced around two legs of the bridle, close up under the seized eyes forming the becket. This should be made fast by a *Rolling Hitch* around the mast wherever you are working. Thus, should any part of the tackle or halyard slip or give way, you will instantly fetch up on the life line with no harm but to your dignity. Furthermore, when tethered in this manner, you can't swing out from the mast when the boat rolls. Should you be working on the spreader-tips it is not necessary to hold on with one hand—just transfer the *Rolling Hitch* to the upper shroud just above the spreader and both hands are free. Finally, there's the peace of mind that comes from knowing that the lifeline makes you doubly secure, as safe aloft as down on deck.

Before taking off "into the wild blue yonder" it is advisable to give some thought to the problem of carrying aloft the miscellaneous tools needed for the particular job you are about to tackle. The natural inclination is to stow them in your pockets and about your person, but experience has proven this to be a very unsatisfactory practice, a fact to which I can honestly attest.

For years I habitually crammed my pockets full of tools, and one by one, year after year I saw them slip out, drop to the deck and bounce overboard. For years I carried cans of spar enamel tenderly aloft by the bail, and discovered I could get far more coverage by dropping the can than I ever could with a brush. Many a needless trip have I made 'twixt masthead and deck for the forgotten pliers or the right-size wrench. In view of such lubberly blundering it is small wonder that things came to a spectacular climax and I learned the error of my ways.

On a hot summer day I had gone aloft to rig a new spring-stay, garbed only in a pair of dungarees, the pockets of which I had stuffed with tools, as usual. From the dock close by a sizable crowd of picnickers watched my every move while they waited for the ferry. I was having trouble removing a cotter-pin from the masthead fitting I could barely reach, and finally got the brilliant idea of standing up in the boatswain's chair. With a death grip on the masthead I eased out of the seat, and as I drew myself erect my belt parted, and my overloaded dungarees dropped to my feet! Bare as a bell buoy, and with the raucous cries of the multitude ringing in my burning ears, it took some alarming acrobatics to retrieve my pants while holding on with one hand.

When safely on deck once more I knew I had had

enough, and swore I wouldn't go aloft again until I was properly equipped. Out of that embarrassing experience came the idea for the handy rigger's bucket I have here illustrated, and it has proven to be such a perfect little helper that I can't understand why I didn't think of it sooner.

The bail is a toggle-and-becket, which is buttoned to one leg of the boatswain's chair. A rope grommet is enclosed in the rim of the bucket as a stiffener to keep it open, and it has a wooden bottom. All the commonly needed tools fit snugly in the loops around the outside, in plain sight and easy to get at without pawing around. Inside the bucket I stow the marline, wire seizing stuff, spare shackles, cotter-pins, oil can and grease. When painting or varnishing the spars the quart can sits securely in the bucket, and if it should slop over there's no danger of messing up the decks below.

For practice in splicing, serving and sewing with the palm and needle the making of this bucket is an ideal project, a pleasant task to while away a rainy afternoon. You'll need a piece of 10 ounce canvas about 11 by 24 inches, some tarred hemp rope and a disk of ½ inch pine or mahogany 7 inches in diameter, the bucket being 7 by 9 inches.

The first step is to place the canvas in position around the wooden bottom, with a 1 inch flat seam allowed for, and the raw edges of the canvas turned under. Mark the position of the seam carefully with a pencil, then take it off and sew both sides of the seam with the *flat stitch*.

With a single strand of ⅜ inch rope 69 inches long, lay up a grommet 7 inches in diameter. Place it inside the top and turn the canvas down to make a 1½ inch seam, then sew it down with the flat seam stitch. Two *worked holes* should now be made in the seam close under the rope grommet and opposite each other.

Now turn the canvas inside out, to bring the top seam on the *inside* of the bucket. Work the lower edge carefully over the wood bottom, turning the canvas under ¼ inch to hide the raw edge, and fasten with ⅜ inch copper tacks placed an inch apart.

The two legs of the bail are now spliced into the holes and served over. One terminates in a spliced-in toggle and the other in a spliced eye. The toggle can be easily made from a ⅜ inch wood dowel 1½ inches long, with tapered ends and a groove at the center to take the rope.

The bucket is now complete except for the looped band of canvas to hold the tools. It should be a doubled strip, 1½ inches wide, and securely sewn. The size of the loops and their spacing can only be determined by placing your tools in position, one by one, and marking the canvas. As to just what tools to include, you alone can decide. I have found that the ones most needed are a screwdriver, roundnose pliers, wire cutting pliers, marlinspike, and a small adjustable end wrench.

At fitting-out time in the Spring you'll find this little tool carrier mighty handy for use on deck as well as aloft. Take it with you wherever you're working and everything you need is ready at hand.

XX

Rope-Strapped Blocks

For a year or more before the keel of the *Morning Star* was laid I spent many long hours in my workshop making the innumerable fittings, hardware and gear I had dreamed about so long. Above the workbench hung two massive, rope-strapped blocks that had worn themselves out on a coasting schooner long before I was born. Their rust-pitted sheaves rattled on worn pins, their scarred and bleached oak shells still bore traces of green paint, and their hempen straps were frayed and chafed nearly half through. Homely and unadorned, they were a far cry from the beautifully finished gear of a yacht and would seem to hold but little in the way of inspiration.

But whenever I lifted my eyes from my work I would find those two old blocks staring at me forlornly, intruding on my thoughts and setting me to dreaming. For upwards of five hundred years ships were fitted with rope-strapped blocks, this I knew; yet here in the middle of the twentieth century they were practically obsolete —why? If they were so obviously practical through all those centuries why shouldn't they be equally useful today? Why not on the *Morning Star?*

Why not, indeed! From the meadows I retrieved an old, well-seasoned locust fence post that I had long had my eye on, and after rounding up some bronze sheaves and round stock for pins I set about making a complete set of blocks for jib, main and mizzen. *Gosh!* thought I, *sailors have more fun than people!* With the enthusiasm born of discovery the work proceeded apace and I soon had a row of golden locust shells gleaming with six coats of varnish. When the last tarred hemp strap had been seized in place and the blocks were lined up for inspection I paid a silent tribute to the crude relics on the wall for their inspiration. These simple, handmade affairs that I had turned out with so little effort revealed an inherent beauty and a distinctive character that could never be found in their modern, highly-engineered counterparts.

It is now six years since these blocks were installed in my little ship, and I am mightily proud of them. Wherever we have sailed they have been examined, handled and admired by countless visitors. They recognize them as a symbol of the age of sail—romantic reminders of the ancient arts of the sailor, and few can resist their appeal.

But it is not for their historical interest or romantic appeal that I am here concerned—it is their practical adaptation to modern needs. After six years experience with rope-strapped blocks I am convinced that they are in some respects superior to metal blocks, and I feel amply justified in recommending their use. In fact I am so prejudiced in their favor that, save for one or two exceptions, I will use nothing else henceforth.

In the first place, they are noticeably light in weight in comparison with metal or composite yacht blocks. Secondly, they are infinitely *quieter,* an attribute of considerable importance in cruising yachts. Their rope straps act as built-in fenders, cushioning the impact as they slat and bang against the deck or spars. If properly shaped they are perfectly streamlined and never foul or catch on sheets, halyards or other gear. This is especially important when they are used for jibsheets. Finally, there are no exposed metal parts to corrode and tarnish —just the ageless beauty of hempen rope and varnished wood!

Space does not permit me to pursue the subject exhaustively, as I am sorely tempted, nor do I intend to show you how to become a professional block-maker. My only desire is to direct your interest, to point the way that you may design and make your own, improvising and adapting to suit your particular requirements, just as I have done. To this end, therefore, it is important to know some of the background of this ancient sailor's art.

In the days when they were in common use, rope-strapped blocks were of infinite variety. Fitted with common beckets, rope tails, slings, hooks, or toggles-and-beckets, each was devised for a specific application. In size they ran from a bare 2 inches for awning tackles up to enormous 24 inch "heaving down" blocks with 4 sheaves. The shells of the blocks were of two kinds— *morticed,* which were cut from a single piece of wood, and *made,* in which the cheeks were riveted through spacers. Only the smaller blocks were of the morticed type.

They were made of various woods; ash, oak, locust, madeira, ironwood or lignum vitae—in fact, any hard, close-grained wood that was readily at hand. I have seen small blocks made of whale bone and they were beautiful. Naturally enough, they were from whale ships.

In their earlier form the sheaves were often of wood, although iron was more common, and they had simple bushings. Roller bushings of various kinds were used in the later types, with the possible exception of relatively small blocks for light work.

Tarred hemp rope was used for strapping, generally wormed, parcelled and served, and frequently re-tarred to keep out moisture and prevent rot. The strap would be in the form of a grommet, or a short splice might be used, with the splice at the breech or bottom of the block. Wire straps were sometimes used in later years, parcelled, wormed and tarred.

The shells were painted white, green or black—never varnished, except in naval craft. White blocks with their tarred straps were quite effective accents, and a well-kept ship fairly sparkled with them. Many of our early yachts had rope-strapped blocks, even though composite "yacht blocks" were then available, but they were varnished in keeping with the traditional bright-work that was common to all pleasure craft.

I have shown among the accompanying illustrations working drawings for a simple, single-sheave, morticed block to take ⅜ inch rope. Should you desire to design

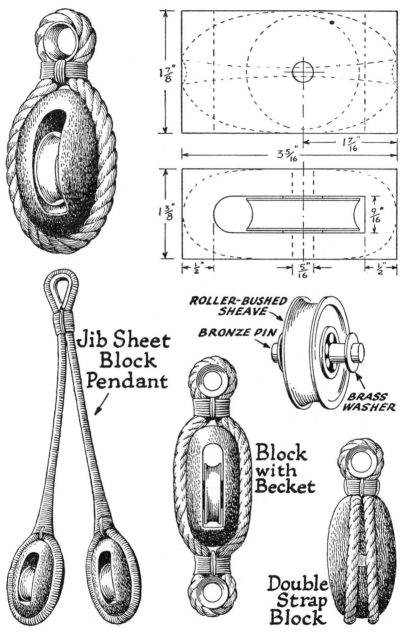

$1\frac{7}{8}''$

$1\frac{7}{16}''$

$3\frac{5}{16}''$

$1\frac{3}{8}''$

$\frac{9}{16}''$

$\frac{1}{2}''$ $\frac{5}{16}''$ $\frac{1}{2}''$

ROLLER-BUSHED SHEAVE

BRONZE PIN

BRASS WASHER

Jib Sheet Block Pendant

Block with Becket

Double Strap Block

171

your own, perhaps for a larger rope or a double block, the dimensions given will serve as a starting point. I can strongly recommend that you stick to the morticed type, for few amateurs have the skill and craftsmanship necessary to turn out a creditable *made* block.

As to the choice of wood, I would stick to locust or mahogany, close, straight-grained and well-seasoned. If you prefer mahogany be sure it is *real* mahogany, the hard kind, and not the soft, cigar-box type which is actually a variety of cedar.

Lay out the squared blank carefully and scribe the center lines, mortice, and pin position accurately. A drill press should be used to insure that the mortice and pin hole are precisely at right angles to the blank and to each other. A file is a great help in fairing up the mortice.

When the blank has been thus bored and morticed it should be roughed to finished shape with a wood rasp and finished up with sandpaper. Care must be used here, for if you take a little too much off near the ends, the block will be weakened at each end of the mortice. The shallow groove to take the strap is made with a rat-tail file, deepest at the ends and fading out to nothing at the pin hole. Two coats of varnish go on when the shell is finished, and since it will be marred up somewhat in putting on the strap, the finished coats are applied when the strap is finally seized in place.

Bronze sheaves are obtainable either plain or roller bushed. You will notice that I have specified a $1\frac{3}{4}$ inch sheave. This is the minimum diameter that should be used with $\frac{3}{8}$ inch rope—2 inch would be much better, and the block must be made ¼ inch wider to accommodate it. The purpose of the brass washers is to prevent the sheave from riding on the sides of the mortice. The bronze pin must fit the hole tightly, otherwise it would turn with the sheave.

Only tarred hemp rope, not less than ⅜ inch in diameter, should be used for the strap—under no circumstances use manila. Hemp is used because it has so little stretch, and since it is tarred there is no danger of rot. I do not recommend worming, parcelling and serving the strap for blocks as small as this, mainly because it takes a lot of experience to be able to estimate the exact size to make the strap before the service is applied. However, if you are willing to gamble the time it would take to re-make and re-serve the strap it is worth doing. Unfortunately there is no way to tell whether the strap is the right size until it is completely served over, other than by trial and error.

The block that I have shown is called an *eye block,* since it has an eye with a common brass sail-thimble seized in, to take a shackle or hook. With the thimble held in position at the top of the block, the strap should fit tightly, *before* the seizing is clapped on. The strap is a grommet—with the tucked ends placed at the bottom of the block. The short-spliced strap that I mentioned earlier should only be used on much larger blocks as it is clumsy and not so neat in appearance.

When the strap is ready to be seized on, pack the sheave bushing with water pump grease, place in position with its washers and press the pin in. The ends of the pin should be flush with the sides of the block, and don't worry about it dropping out, for the strap holds it securely

Place the strap in position, and if it is the proper size it should take considerable effort to force the thimble into place. Italian tarred marline is used for the round seizing, which should consist of about eight initial turns and one less riding turns, finished off with two to four crossing turns and a reef knot. This seizing must be as tight as you can possibly make it, for it is all that prevents your block from literally falling apart. Now the only way to get it tight enough is as follows. Grease the marline thoroughly and put on the first layer of turns hand taut. With the inactive end held in the left hand, take a marlinspike hitch with the working part about the tip of your marlinspike, close to the seizing, and by using the tool as a lever heave the seizing tight. Then holding all your gain put on the riding turns hand taut.

Right about now you should be ready for a drink or a smoke, or both, for the first block is more difficult to make than the second or third. It is somewhat like having babies, or opening a bottle of olives—after you get the first the rest come easy. With a couple of finishing coats of varnish your block is now ready for use. By the end of its first season, or sooner depending upon the amount of service, you will find that the strap has stretched and is loose on the block. This calls for a new seizing to take up the slack, and henceforth the block must be inspected at regular intervals for the condition of the seizing. I have found that after the initial stretching of the first season the strap stays put, but nevertheless I replace the seizing every 2 years as a matter of precaution, and re-pack the bushing with waterproof grease at the same time.

This, plus the annual revarnishing is the only service these blocks require, although I can conceive that eventually the straps might become chafed and brittle with age and have to be renewed. In fact the strapping, reseizing and tarring of blocks was normal routine in the days of sail and the techniques involved were far more complicated than those I have just described.

Present day yacht blocks are made with a large variety of fittings for numerous applications. With a little ingenuity rope strapped blocks can be made to meet the same requirements, and with that in mind I have shown a few practical modifications.

In the block I have described you will note that the thimble is at right angles to the sheave, and there are certain applications where this arrangement would not be suitable. Should you require that the thimble and the sheave lie in the same plane this can be accomplished by using a *doubled strap* as I have shown. Obviously the block will need two parallel grooves to take the strap. *All double blocks,* and single blocks bearing a heavy load should have *doubled straps.* If the block must have a becket to take the standing part of the fall, seize in another thimble at the base of the block as shown.

I have also shown a jib sheet block pendant as another adaptation. The bight of the pendant is seized around a thimble for shackling to the clew, and the pendant ends are spliced around the blocks. It would be difficult to make the eye splice fit the block tightly enough, so it is best to have a loose fit and depend on a round seizing

about the neck of the splice to draw it up taut. The pendant should by all means be parcelled and served over,
for there is considerable chafe. It would be advisable
to use wire rope rather than hemp if the jib sheets are
larger than ⅜ inch.

It may seem odd to find the next item classed as a rope

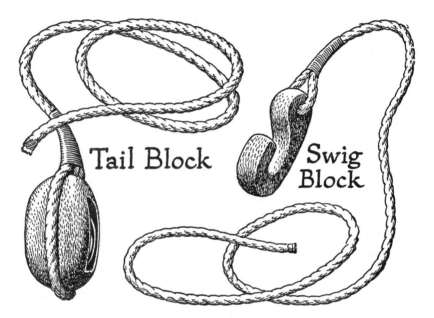

Tail Block   Swig Block

strapped block, but a *swig block* actually is a snatch block
without a sheave. It is a very old form used exclusively
to set up lashings, primarily in whaleships, and generally
was made of whalebone. In the small yacht it is a very
handy piece of gear to prevent the annoying slat of halyards against the mast when lying at anchor. The block
is hooked on to the halyard as high as you can reach and
the lanyard is set up to a shroud, thus holding the hal-

yard clear of everything. The blocks are 2 inches long, of varnished mahogany, and the light cotton lanyards are about 4 feet in length.

The *tail block* is designed to be made fast to standing rigging or to spars. It is simplicity itself—a few feet of hemp rope spliced around the block with a round seizing. In my opinion its best application is in connection with light sails. Often it is desired to trim the sheet of a balloon jib or balloon staysail to the main or mizzen boom, more or less temporarily. In a matter of seconds a tail block can be secured to the boom with a rolling hitch, whereas, with a modern yacht block you always have to first locate a spare piece of line for a lashing, then make fast to both the block and the boom. The old-fashioned tail block is quicker, more convenient and complete in itself.

There are many more ways of strapping and adapting these blocks, but I think I have demonstrated their infinite possibilities, and by your own ingenuity you can work out many arrangements to suit your own taste and requirements. I can assure you that your efforts will not have been in vain, for the appealing character they possess cannot be ignored by any true sailor—theirs is a beauty that cannot be purchased in a store!

XXI

On the Making of Rope Mats

When I was a boy it was my good fortune to be a frequent visitor in the homes of many seafaring men by virtue of their friendship with my elders. They were masters of yachts and merchant ships, coasting schooners and fishermen, and some were just plain clam diggers. But however varied their careers might have been and whatever the state of their fortunes, their homes all had one thing in common—some distinguishing feature that revealed unmistakably their owners' calling.

There was the two-masted schooner with her mains'l up, swinging to a fresh sou'wester a-top the barn; the weather-beaten cabin trunk from the old *Ella C.*, still giving service as a chicken-coop; or the old iron try-pot on the front lawn filled with red geraniums.

Indoors your roving eye would note the chart-track of *Katrina's* cruise to the Mediterranean in '88, neatly framed on the wall beside a fine old French barometer; the quaintly decorated whale's tooth on the mantel; or the apple-green sea chest filled with blankets in the upstairs hall.

But of all these things I knew and loved none are more

178

vividly remembered than the curious rope mat that bespoke a simple welcome at each doorstep. Here indeed was the trademark, the one infallible sign announcing to all who entered that here lived a sailor, for nowhere else on shore would you be likely to come upon a sample of this ancient sailor's art.

Many of these rope mats were but a simple Flemish coil, and some were embellished with a decorative flat knot in the center. They might be round or elliptical, or a rectangular Sword mat. I remember an elaborate oval mat with a handsome border design in the form of a running wave, brought ashore from some long-forgotten yacht.

With a boy's peculiar sense of values, I somehow came to judge a man's importance by the quality of his doormat. I always rated "Uncle" Frank a bit higher than Capt. Tom Hawkins because he sported a fancier mat, although his magnificent swearing might have been a factor. Ironically "Uncle" Frank was a clam digger all his life, while Capt. Tom had commanded China tea clippers and had roamed the Seven Seas. But Capt. Crosby outshone them all—he was a man set apart. *He* had a rope mat on the floor of his privy!

For hundreds of years rope mats of various types were primarily used as chafing gear in sailing ships, commonly laced to the spars to take the chafe of the standing rigging when braced up sharp on the wind. They were nailed to the rails at vulnerable points, they cushioned the deck from the rattle and bang of blocks and provided a skid-proof footing for the helmsman. Companionways, thresholds and gangways, all received this handsome, decorative protection. Small wonder indeed that the sailor brought them ashore to his doorstep!

Before the turn of the century rope mats were to be found on every well-kept yacht the world over. Old photographs of deck scenes reveal their many uses and attest to their universal popularity. But in more recent times they have been sadly neglected by the yachtsman, more's the pity, and today they are rarely seen.

Just why so simple a thing as the making of rope mats should suddenly become a lost art is hard to understand, for they are unquestionably useful, inexpensive and easily made. Aesthetically, I know of no single item of traditionally-correct ship's gear that is more fitting and appropriate, or that does so much to give a yacht character and personality. From the standpoint of utility they protect the decks from wear and tear where traffic is heaviest, and in wet weather when one's footing is precarious they grip the deck stubbornly without slipping. Finally, they require an investment of nothing more than a few hours' time since they are made from rope that has been used and discarded.

In the smaller cruising yacht I would earnestly recommend a rope mat in the cockpit for the helmsman to stand on, another at the threshold of the companionway to keep sand and dirt from getting below deck, and one at the foot of the ladder to absorb some of the water from dripping oilskins. A strip of Sword mat several feet long on each side-deck gives sure footing to anyone coming aboard and prevents unsightly scars from high-heeled shoes or hobnailed brogans.

The simplest mat to make is the round or elliptical Flemish coil. The rope is first laid out and overhauled to eliminate all twists and turns, for unless it lays absolutely fair the mat will not lie flat, particularly when wet. It is then coiled carefully, the turns lying close and smooth, with even tension throughout. Additional rope should be joined with a long splice if it is needed. Then the turns of the coil are stitched together with a single length of marline threaded in a large sail needle. There are several ways to do this.

You may use the *herringbone stitch* (see chapter on *Hand Sewing and Canvaswork*), which is tedious and time-consuming but most secure. Or you may prefer the simple overhand stitch I have illustrated, which progresses quite rapidly. Although it is possible to sew the turns together *as you coil the rope,* it generally results in a distorted, lumpy mat that may not lie flat. If the herringbone stitch is used the mat will of course be turned over so the stitches cannot be seen, but with the overhand stitch the marline can be sunk beneath the surface between the strands, and the mat may be used either side up.

In my estimation the plain Flemish coil above, while entirely practical, is too plain and uninteresting, suggesting that its maker was an indolent individual with no imagination. But put a simple decorative flat knot in the center as I have shown and it immediately becomes a thing of beauty and character. I cannot understand why so many men back off in alarm at the first suggestion that they tackle a decorative knot. I'll agree that some of them appear intricate and involved at first

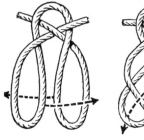   

The Flemish Coil Mat
with Ocean Plat Knot

**Sewing the Turns
with Marline**

glance, but I have yet to see *any* knot, so matter how involved, that a 12-year-old child couldn't tie on the first attempt if given a proper set of simple diagrams. So let's have no nonsense about a fancy mat being too difficult!

The decorative knot I have shown here is known as the *Ocean Plat,* and the rope used in making it should be one size smaller than that used for the Flemish coil, for since the parts across one another its thickness is doubled and it would otherwise be a bit bulky. Thus, if you are using ½ inch rope for the coil the knot should be made of ⅜ inch.

To the best of my recollection it takes about 35 feet of ⅜ inch rope to make this knot, triple-passed. Start with a bight about 12 or 14 feet from one end and lay it up loosely as shown in the three diagrams. This will leave you with a short end and a long one. Enter the long end alongside of the short end where it emerges and pass it through the knot making a complete circuit, and repeat once more. Except that it will be loose and perhaps lopsided, it should look like the finished knot I have shown. So starting with a bight anywhere in the knot, take up the slack all around, working in both directions, until the parts lie close together and the knot is symmetrical. The ends should be whipped and stitched to an adjacent part on the under side.

With the knot completed the Flemish coil is made up about it as described previously. The knot itself will hold together without any sewing, but it must be stitched to the coil where it touches. The knot may be smoothed

The Sword Mat

Thump Mat

Ladder-step Mat

184

up a bit by pounding it with a wooden mallet, but it will flatten out satisfactorily with use.

The *Sword Mat* I have shown here is the oldest form of mat weaving known to man, having but a simple warp and filler. While it cannot be termed fancy, it is an excellent deck covering where a square-cornered mat is wanted, and can be made in any proportion to fit the available space. It is particularly useful on the narrow side decks and in passageways down below in the cabin. A narrow strip of it tacked to the rail-cap up forward gives protection where the anchor comes aboard.

The Sword Mat I have shown here has ½ inch rope for the warp and heavy seine twine as the filler. For a mat 15 by 30 inches you would need 30 pieces of rope 60 inches long, and about 70 feet of twine. Middle the 30 pieces of rope over a head-rope about 2 feet long, lay it all down carefully on the floor. Stretch the head-rope taut and secure it to the floor with a nail at each end. Middle the seine twine and make up each half in a ball or skein. Now lay each alternate rope up over the head rope and then lay the bight of the twine across the other parts, close up into the crotch. The diagram shows this first step.

Now bring the ropes that were laid up over the head-rope back down to their original position, and lay the *other* set up. Carry each skein of twine across to the opposite side close to the crotch, as shown in the second diagram.

If you will hold the marline on one side by putting your foot on it, it can be held taut with one hand, thus leaving the other hand free to lay the ropes up and down.

I think the diagrams and illustration are sufficiently simple to follow without further explanation—just continue laying up alernate sets of strands and crossing the twine each time. Sufficient tension must be maintained on the twine to hold the parts snugly together, or a loose, flimsy mat will result. After the last crossing the ends of the seine twine should be tied together with a square knot. The rope ends should be paired off and secured with a *round seizing.*

The mat may now be removed from the floor and the ends of the headrope finished off with a simple *wall-and-crown knot,* which has been shown in a previous chapter. I neglected to mention that the headrope should not be larger than ¼ inch in diameter, otherwise the wall-and-crown knots would be so large that they would protrude above the surface of the mat.

There are several other forms of rope mats which have an entirely different texture and character, notably the Punch or Wrought Mat and the Walled Mat. They are more difficult to make, consume more time and require a helper in the process. Since this is not a book of knots *per se,* and because the mats I have shown amply cover the needs of the average small yacht, I am omitting any discussion of their construction. Should you wish to pursue the subject further information may be had in any good book on Knots.

Another handsome and practical addition to any yacht is the *Thump,* or *Block Mat.* Deck blocks habitually bang and clatter annoyingly every time you shift tacks, scarring bright decks and wearing through canvas covered decks. A thump mat of white cotton or nylon rope placed over the eye-bolt to which the block is secured will absorb the shock of each impact, and its extremely decorative appearance will win the admiration of every visitor on board.

For this mat either laid or braided rope may be used, not less than 1/4 inch or more than 3/8 inch in diameter. It is nothing more than a 3-strand *Turk's Head* knot flattened out. So turn to the chapter on *Decorative Knots* and lay up the knot as described. Tie it quite loosely, then flatten it out on the table and gradually draw up the slack until it is tight and compact. Hide the ends on the under side and secure with a few stitches of sail twine.

Slip it over the eye-bolt on the deck, shackle on your block and you'll have greatly improved the appearance of your yacht. Under no circumstance should you use manila rope for this one—only a *white* rope can bring out its inherent beauty!

My last mat is for the companion ladder steps, and is also made with white cotton rope. It is known very fittingly as the *Sailor's True Lover Mat Weave,* and is made in much the same manner as the *Ocean Plat* previously described.

Just lay it up carefully as in the diagrams here shown, observing the over-and-under sequence and keeping it loose. Pass an end in a complete circuit around the knot, keeping always on the same side of the rope you are following, and repeat, thus there are three passes in all. Take out the slack until it is snug and symmetrical, hide the ends and stitch them fast underneath, and finally secure the finished mat to the ladder step with brass escutcheon pins.

It should take no more than a half-hour to complete one of these mats once you have become familiar with the sequence, so a complete set is not much of a chore.

XXII

How to Make a Proper Bucket

If there is one subject on which I am violently opinionated it is the matter of a proper deck bucket. In fact, just sitting here thinking about it makes me hot under the collar, for I have had so much experience with the *wrong* kind.

Most yachtsmen seem to think that a galvanized pail with a rope tied to the bail is a proper bucket, just as I once did. Now I'll admit that a tin pail is a handy though uncomfortable substitute for a marine toilet, but as a deck bucket for a respectable yacht it is a curse and abomination, and the man who started the fad should have been boiled in oil in one.

For years I sailed with a tin pail in an 18 foot day sailer, and while it was very useful in an emergency what it did to my nerves was a caution. With space at a premium the only place I could stow it was in the forepeak, and in beating to windward in a good breeze every time the bow smacked into a wave with a *bang,* there was an answering *clang* from the pail. I would spare one hand from the tiller and ram it with an oar, and it would be quiet for about ten waves, then that damn clanging would resume. When it was time to get the anchor and cable up on deck I would crawl up for-'ard on my belly and back out the same way, and the cussed pail would follow right along, fouled in the cable or the anchor fluke. Finally I sold the boat, and with it went the pail, and as far as I know it's still clanging away to every wave slap and making life miserable for the present owner.

Then came the building of the *Morning Star,* and the dawn of a new era—33 feet on deck and stowage space galore. With the thousand and one details of fitting out, a deck bucket was the least of my worries, and finally the day of the maiden voyage was at hand. With the new motor throttled down to a quiet purr we slipped down the creek and out into the bay, intending to get the feel of the boat under power before setting the sails. When well clear of the breakwater I leaned forward and opened the throttle, and instantaneously there arose a loud, tinny clattering that sounded like no motor I had ever heard. For a frightened instant I thought the gas tank had come adrift, but the noise was from the *other* side of the cockpit. I yanked open the door of the locker under the deck and there in all its pristine glory sat a shiny, new galvanized pail! Some well-meaning but misguided friend had smuggled it aboard when I wasn't around.

Right then I decided that at the first opportunity I was going to make a *proper* deck bucket, a *sailor's* bucket fit for a decent boat, and be forever free from shoreside tinware. From that decision came the sea-going, old style canvas bucket I have shown here, and it has brought me peace and contentment at long last. It doesn't leave dents in everything it touches, or mar your topsides and brightwork. It doesn't require several cubic feet of your best locker—it stows flat like an opera hat. But most important of all it is quiet as a clam in a mudhole—it doesn't make a sound!

One of the nicest things about making your own gear, aside from pride of ownership, is that it affords an opportunity to get in some practice in the sailor's arts. In the making of this bucket you'll do some hand sewing, some roping, a few splices and a fancy knot, and you'll have gained some experience and had pleasure to boot. What more could you ask?

The canvas for this bucket should be heavy weight, no lighter than number 12 duck, so that when filled with water it will stand up stiff and straight without collapsing. You'll need a piece about 15 by 31 inches, which makes a bucket 9½ inches in diameter by 12 inches deep.

The first step is to get out the wooden bottom. Cut a circular disk of ½ inch white or red cedar exactly 9½ inches in diameter, and give it 3 coats of varnish or white paint. Using this as a guide, place the canvas about the circumference and mark it for size, allowing for a flat seam 1 inch or 1¼ inches wide, with the edges turned under ¼ inch. Now put the bottom aside for a while and sew up the flat seam, using a double length of sail twine, well waxed, and keeping your stitches fairly close together—about 5 to the inch.

To keep the bucket from caving in at the rim when lifting it filled with water it is necessary to provide some sort of stiffening, and the traditional way is to inclose a

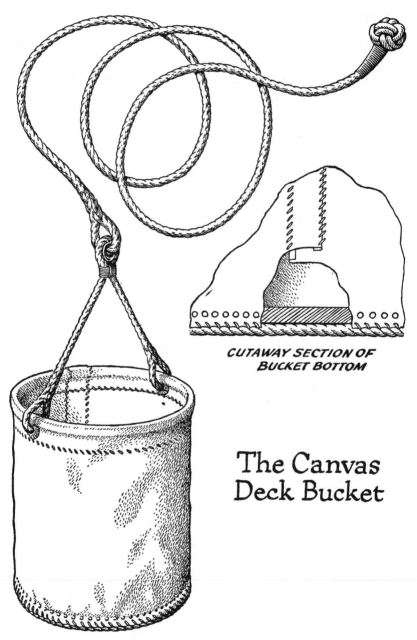

CUTAWAY SECTION OF
BUCKET BOTTOM

The Canvas
Deck Bucket

wooden mast hoop in the seam at the top. If you can't obtain a new or used hoop the proper size (9 inch), you can steam-bend a piece of ash or white oak ⅜ by ¾ inches, scarphing the ends and riveting them together. If you are still stymied, it is permissible to use a grommet of ½ inch rope—tarred hemp if you can get it, manila if you can't. Because of its rigidity the wooden hoop is preferable, and the bucket holds its shape better. But after all, I'm only describing the perfect bucket and you may improvise to suit your fancy.

With your hoop or grommet placed about the top, turn the canvas down over it, outside, making the seam a full 1½ inches deep, and sew it fast with the flat stitch. On opposite sides in this hem make the worked eyelets to take the bail, and these eyelets should be large enough to admit a ⅜ inch rope.

Now make up a grommet of ⅜ inch tarred hemp boltrope (obtainable from your sailmaker), exactly 9½ inches in diameter outside. Turn the bucket upside down and drop the wooden bottom inside. Place the rope grommet inside the canvas, turn the raw edge of the cloth under ¼ inch, and sew it in place, using the roping stitch described in the chapter on *Handsewing* and *Canvaswork*.

Turn the bucket rightside up again and work the wooden bottom down until it is firmly and squarely seated on the rope grommet. Now tack the canvas to the bottom all around, using ⅜ inch copper tacks spaced ½ inch or less apart.

For the bail, or becket, middle a length of ⅜ inch rope around a ¾ inch brass sail thimble and clap on a *round seizing.* Splice the ends into the eyelets in the rim of the bucket taking care to see that the two legs are the same length.

The bucket rope should be $\frac{1}{2}$ inch manila, and its finished length not less than 5 feet, thus you'll require about 7 feet. Splice one end into the thimble eye of the bail, then measure off 5 feet and clap on a stout seizing of marline, preferably a *Constrictor Knot.* Now unlay the rope end to the seizing, put a temporary whipping or stopping on each strand, and proceed to tie the best damn *Manrope Knot* you are capable of, to keep the rope from ever slipping through your hand and prevent the loss of the best deck bucket you ever owned!

After stenciling the name of your ship on the side you'll be anxious to try it out. Toss it over the side to fill it and notice that it hits the water with a respectable *thump* instead of a *clang.* Haul off and slosh a bucketful along the side deck and observe how the rope grommet at the bottom provides a perfect handhold. Or set the filled bucket on a varnished hatch cover and note that the same grommet serves as a perfect fender for the bottom. Then when you're through using it throw it nonchalantly into the cockpit—it can't hurt a thing. Now *jump* on it and smack it flat—it's only a bare 3 inches high now and no problem to stow. But above all else, praise God, you'll never hear a sound out of it!

XXIII

How to Make and Use a Heaving Line

The heaving line has been described as "a light line weighted at its end to aid in throwing to a pier or another vessel, as a messenger for a heavy line." It is commonly employed in all commercial craft as an aid in docking, but its use in yachts has been sadly neglected, and more's the pity, for there are times when it is a mighty handy piece of gear to have on board.

While a yacht but rarely needs a heaving line in docking, it is a great help in putting a line aboard a distressed vessel—the capsized sailboat, the disabled motorboat, or the yacht aground. A coil of rope stout enough for a towline can be thrown a very short distance even under the most ideal conditions, and in heavy weather it is often too dangerous, or even impossible to approach close enough to the disabled craft; but a proper heaving line can be "shot" upwards of 50 feet, even against the wind, with a high degree of accuracy. This is possible because of the weighted knot in the end of the line, which acts in a sense like a projectile.

The Monkey's Fist is the traditional heaving line

knot, its spherical shape and bulk making it ideal for the purpose. But bulk alone is not enough—it must be weighted to achieve the desired distance and accuracy by enclosing within it a ball of some sort—of rubber, wood or metal as your fancy dictates. A ball of lead has often been used, but since it then becomes a lethal weapon to the man who tries to catch it there's a question of how much weight is sporting. I prefer a ball of wood or rubber, since it will float if it lands in the water. This is quite important when the heaving line is thrown to a man overboard, for otherwise the line would quickly sink out of sight.

The ideal heaving line is from 60 to 75 feet long, of 5/16 diameter manila, well broken in. By *broken in* I mean free of all tendency to kink, and with the initial stretch worked out. This can be done by stretching the new rope up between two trees and leaving it there a few days.

To tie the Monkey's Fist Knot, take a bight of the rope about 4 feet from the end and put 3 turns around the extended fingers of the left hand, as shown in the first sketch. Now pass the working end between the fingers and take 3 frapping turns around the first set of turns, as shown in the next two sketches. Remove the knot from the left hand and by passing the end *through* the knot take 3 turns about the second set, inside the first set of turns, as shown in the fourth sketch.

With the knot thus set up loosely, it is necessary to loosen it still more to admit the ball or weight. I use a wooden ball 1½ inches in diameter. After inserting the ball you will find it takes considerable adjusting to ar-

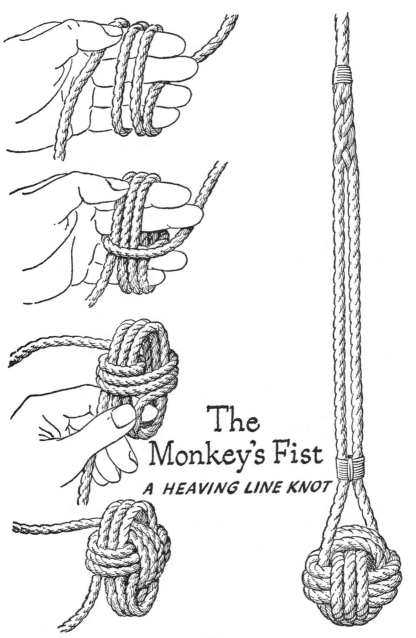

The Monkey's Fist

A HEAVING LINE KNOT

197

range the strands of the knot symmetrically and uniform, and to keep them in place while you take out the slack.

When all is snug and neat the working end, which should be about 2 feet long, must be spliced into the standing part as it lies, fairly. Put a neat seizing about the 2 legs close to the Monkey's Fist and the job is done.

Having completed the heaving line, common sense demands that you step out on the lawn and practice throwing it, to determine whether it has the required weight and to get the feel of it. If it is too light you get neither distance nor accuracy, and it is then necessary to replace the ball with a heavier one. Coil the line in fairly large loops, and with the coil held loosely over the fingers of the left hand, grasp the line with the right hand about 2 feet from the knot. Now swing the rope in a vertical circle by your side so that it leaves your hand in an *underhand* throw. *Don't* swing it around your head like a cowboy. Nothing must obstruct the easy flow of the turns from the coil, and if you throw with some speed or force there is less danger of a "backlash," as it might be called.

Bear in mind that when I speak of accuracy I do not mean that it is necessary to hit a man right between the eyes; *direction* is the important thing, for the idea is to carry the line *across* the disabled boat as near the center as possible, so that it may be readily grabbed by someone on board. While approaching, the bitter end of the heaving line is bent to the end of the heavier working line or cable with a *Sheet Bend* or a *Rolling Hitch,* the latter being preferred if the cable is fairly large or stiff.

Needless to say, the heaving line should be maintained

in a seaman-like fashion, always accessible and neatly coiled. The best way to be sure it is always ready for use is to overhaul and recoil it frequently, and to see that it is used for no other purpose.

XXIV

The Sailor's Ditty Bag

If there is one virtue necessary for the successful operation of the smaller yacht it is orderliness. This is an attribute few possess to the required degree; it must be nurtured and cultivated resolutely, and is achieved only by rigid, determined self-discipline. To the experienced yachtsman, "shipshape" has a very special significance; it denotes an habitual neatness and an exacting standard of personal conduct seldom found ashore.

For the sake of convenience one will toss a coil of rope on the berth instead of carefully stowing it away in the forepeak; tools will be chucked off in the nearest corner, the binoculars on the ice chest and the sun glasses behind the stove. Soon all is confusion and disorder below decks; you can't sit down without first shoving something aside; worse still, when something is needed in a hurry there's a frantic rummaging in all the wrong places betwixt stem and stern. Truly, in such a yacht there is no pleasure.

The only permissible alternative is a planned system of stowage, the dividing of all gear into separate, logical classifications or departments and allotting a permanent place to each. From my own experience I know that it is quite easy to initiate such a system, but to adhere to it is a different matter entirely. Human nature being what it is, it is all too easy to slip back into the old, lubberly disorder, and only by constant, resolute discipline can you overcome this natural weakness.

In the matter of stowage I have found that large, bulky objects are not much of a problem—there is generally but one logical place for them, and they seem to take care of themselves. But the multitudinous variety of small things have a tendency to scatter about and are easily lost or misplaced. The obvious solution is to keep them in a ditty box, chest or bag, depending on their bulk, weight or shape. Thus you have a *portable* container that is easily stowed, with everything together and ready at hand. A small chest with rope handles, of a size to fit an allotted space, provides a better means of keeping hand tools together than a locker, where they are generally scattered about in a clutter, and they may then be brought to wherever you may be working.

The tools used in splicing, serving, whipping, seizing and canvas work, which I prefer to call the marlinspike arts, are a heterogeneous assortment of indispensable small objects that *must* be kept together. They are used frequently, and on most jobs no one tool will suffice— often half a dozen will be brought into play. No better container to hold these tools has been devised than the *Sailor's Ditty Bag*. It is light in weight, may be hung from a hook or stowed 'most anywhere, has a handle for carrying, and there are no hard corners—in short, it is just about perfect.

My own ditty bag is my most cherished possession; it
has been my inseparable shipmate for so many years
that I would feel positively naked without it, and when
I pass over to the Other Shore I want to take it with me
—I aim to spend my eternity worming, parceling and
serving every bar of the pearly gates and finishing them
off with the best damn Turk's Heads I know how to
make!

But more important than the ditty bag itself is what
goes into it. There is no sense in carrying a lot of junk
you rarely need, and you only learn through years of experience just what constitutes a well-equipped kit. With
this in mind I emptied my bag and inventoried its contents. Here are the things I have found to be indispensable:

Sewing palm
Needle case, with *complete* assortment of needles
3 spools of sail twine, fine, medium and coarse
Cake of beeswax
Seam rubber
Bench hook
2 balls of marline, light and heavy
Small serving board
Small ball of seine twine
Tube of Duco cement
Tube of grease
Several coils of Monel seizing wire
Round nose pliers, with wire cutter
Roll of electrician's friction tape
8-inch hickory fid

Handful of assorted manila rope thimbles
Small box of brass cotter pins

With the addition of your sheath knife and marlin-spike, these things are entirely adequate for the normal run of repairs and maintenance on the average small yacht, and in my estimation represent the *minimum* requirements for a well equipped ditty bag.

To the sailor of olden times the ditty bag was as important as his sea chest, and into its making went many an hour off watch. Being a personal item he looked upon it as a means of expression—an opportunity to show how much he had learned of "fancy work." I have examined many old ditty bags, and whether they were simple or elaborate, the workmanship was excellent and revealed their owner's pride in his craft. These bags were 12 to 15 inches deep and from 6 to 8 inches in diameter, with 6 or 8 hand-worked eyelets around the top into which were spliced or seized the legs of the lanyard. No two lanyards were ever alike, for each was designed to suit the sailor's fancy, but most of them had a Turk's Head knot enclosing the legs which was slid up or down to open or close the bag.

The bag I have shown here is quite simple and anyone of average ability should have no difficulty in making it, for all of the skills involved may be found in this book. Use a lightweight canvas, no heavier than 8-ounce, and lay it out as shown in the diagram. This makes a bag 7 inches in diameter by 12 inches deep, with 6 legs to the lanyard.

First lap the two edges of the bag with a flat seam,

turning both raw edges under before stitching, as shown in the chapter on canvaswork. Next fold the top down *outside* and sew it with the flat seam stitch. Sew the bottom piece to the bag with an overhand stitch, keeping the stitches well back from the edge.

Now turn the bag inside out and work the eyelets in the seam at the top, spacing them equally as shown and using small grommets of marline. The bag is now complete and ready for the lanyard.

For the lanyard you'll need 3 pieces of cotton line about 3/32 inches in diameter and about 8 feet long, with a temporary whipping of sail twine on each end. Lay up a 3 strand flat sennit braid, 3 inches long, in the center. (See Chapter XIV). Then middle the sennit and clap on a seizing, thus forming an eye with 6 lines depending from it. With these lines work a 6 strand Matthew Walker's Knot close to the seizing.

Now work a 6 strand *continuous crown sennit* for a distance of 3 inches, and follow with another 6 strand Matthew Walker. Next make up a 5-bight Turk's Head Knot, using ⅛ inch braided cotton (flag halyard stuff), saturate it with shellac or varnish and when dry give it one or two coats of white paint. Reeve the 6 legs of the lanyard through the Turk's Head when it is thoroughly dry and splice or seize them into the eyelets of the bag. The legs should be about 10 inches long.

Your ditty bag is now complete except for stenciling or stitching your initials on the side in the sailor's traditional blue. I'll warrant you'll be as proud of your handiwork as I am of mine, and once it is filled with the proper tools you'll immediately cast your eyes about

1½" FOLDOVER

1" LAP

14"

23½"

The Ditty Bag

7½"

H.G.S.

205

for a job that needs doing . . . and you will find many! One final note of warning—don't hang your bag, or anything else for that matter, on a *thwartship* bulkhead, or you'll soon have no bag and a neatly grooved bulkhead.

XXV

How to Rig Deadeyes and Lanyards

Although this ancient art of the rigger is considered obsolete by many present-day yachtsmen, such is far from true, for deadeyes and lanyards are still being used in all manner of sailing craft, being particularly appropriate in the traditional types—such as the Friendship sloops, the Chesapeake bugeyes, or the skipjacks. While their salty, old-fashioned appearance may have been the factor that has induced more than one sentimental yachtsman to adopt them, from the standpoint of practicability they have sufficient merit in their own right to justify their use in any craft of a suitable type.

There are two reasons why I feel some discussion of this uncommon art is in order: in the first place, specific, authentic information on the subject is not within easy reach of everyone, and secondly, there is a great deal of misunderstanding as to their practical application in the modern yacht.

The principal advantage gained by setting up standing rigging with lanyards is elasticity. This is particularly desirable in yachts that are broad of beam, having high initial stability, and heavily sparred. The resiliency of such a rig makes a yacht easy on her gear, for spars and rigging can flex and give with every sudden strain.

This elasticity of lanyards is so well known that it has led to the false assumption that they have to be continually set up to take up the stretch, and are therefore a constant nuisance. This is definitely not true. Like all fiber ropes, lanyards do have a certain amount of initial stretch when new, and during the first season it might be necessary to set them up twice; but once the initial stretch is worked out and they have "found themselves," they become completely stable and require attention only infrequently.

Lanyard stuff is 3-strand tarred hemp, and can still be had from the better rope manufacturers. Once the lanyards are installed they require yearly re-tarring to keep the weather out and prevent rot, and if they are properly cared for they will last for many years. I have found that when you mention "tar" the average person thinks of the solidified coal tar that must be melted for use. The tar used for lanyards, as well as other shipboard use, is a thin, liquid pine oil, and is obtainable from various makers of marine paints. Fishermen tar their nets with pine tar, and the thinnest grade is used on wooden decks in place of paint.

Deadeyes have long since disappeared from the catalogues of the marine hardware manufacturers, but it is my understanding that they may be had on special order. In many boatyards along the coast you may find old deadeyes salvaged from commercial sailing craft at the time of their decease or conversion to power. Unfortunately they are apt to be only the *upper* deadeyes, taken ashore with the rigging, while the "ironed" lower ones were often left to rot away with the hulk. Thus, many yachtsmen have made their own, using locust when lignum vitae was unobtainable, turning them out on a lathe and boring the holes with a drill press.

But it is not my intention to go into the details of constructing homemade deadeyes, with their innumerable types of ironing and countless dimensions for every size and variety. What I am here concerned with is the proper method of reeving, setting up, securing and maintenance of the lanyards; a method developed through centuries of experience and therefore admitting no deviation. Professional riggers of the old school would insist that there is but one way to rig lanyards, since no one has devised a better one. Such are the dictates of tradition.

The standing end of the lanyard must have a knot, and the proper lanyard knot is the *Matthew Walker*. If you will examine an upper deadeye you will see that the *left hand* hole has a sharp edge to support the lanyard knot, while the other two holes are gouged out or faired to take the lanyard without chafing. Lanyards are always rove right-handed, as rope is coiled. The lanyard knot is at the *inboard* side of the *left hand* hole in the upper deadeye. Thus the knot is at the *forward* side of the starboard deadeyes, and at the *after* side of the port deadeyes.

When the lanyard has been properly rove off the working end will emerge from *right hand* hole of the lower deadeye. It is then brought up and secured to the shroud close to the upper deadeye with a *Lanyard Hitch*, known to some as the *Cow Hitch*, as shown in the illus-

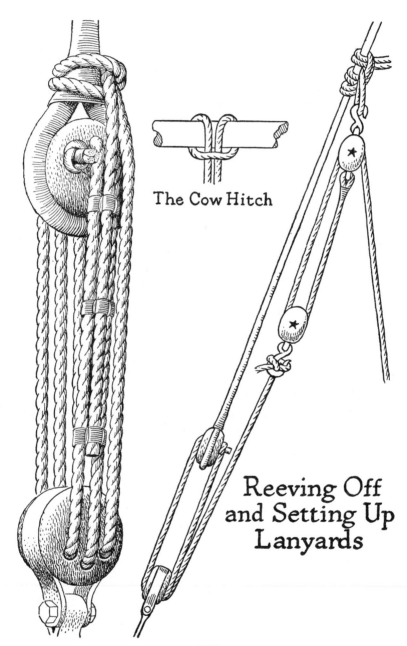

The Cow Hitch

Reeving Off
and Setting Up
Lanyards

tration. The end is now brought down and secured to the *standing part* with 3 round seizings.

But before the lanyard can be secured with the hitch and the seizings it must be set up to get the required tension in the shroud. Bare hands alone will not do the job, and a tackle must be used. Greasing the lanyard and the holes beforehand is advisable as it makes the lanyard render through the deadeyes easily and reduces the friction, which is quite considerable. For a tackle use a *single purchase* (2 single blocks).

Middle a short piece of rope and secure it to the shroud as high up as you can reach with a *Rolling Hitch,* and to this strop, hook the upper block of the tackle. Bend the end of the lanyard to the hook of the lower block with a *Becket Hitch.* Now haul away on your tackle until the shroud has the desired tension, and while you hold all your gain have a helper put several temporary seizings on the standing parts to prevent the lanyard from slipping. Then cast off your tackle and secure the lanyard with the hitch and the permanent seizings.

This is the traditional way of setting up lanyards, and the only variations are in the arrangement of the tackle, large vessels requiring a more complicated system of greater power.

When deadeyes and lanyards are used, the standing rigging is generally galvanized iron or plow steel, parcelled and served throughout its length. All shrouds on a side should be the same length; that is, the upper deadeyes must be perfectly aligned, the same height from the deck. Sheer poles—iron rods about ½ inch in diameter

—are generally secured to the shroud doublings at the upper deadeyes with *flat seizings,* to tie the whole works together and keep the deadeyes neatly in line. Very often the sheer poles are eliminated and a wooden member called a *pin rack,* about 2 by 3 inches for a yacht under 45 feet, is bolted to the shrouds just above the deadeyes and bored to take belaying pins. This is a very handy arrangement for gaff-rigged yachts that do not have a pin rail around the mast, as it keeps the coils of running rigging off the deck and out of the way.

To restate the case for deadeyes and lanyards, they are entirely practical *providing* the yacht is of a suitable type of hull and rig. Obviously they would look rather silly on a racing sloop such as a 6-metre or International, but they are very appropriate for a gaff-rigged, heavily built cruising yacht of a traditional hull type, for they have a character in keeping with such a craft. The elasticity of lanyards is very noticeable when sailing close-hauled in rough weather in a burdensome yacht that is stiff on her feet. You can actually feel the flexing of the whole rig—quite distinct from the jarring snap one usually expects, and if you should go aloft you would discover that the lanyards are actually a sort of sea-going shock absorbers. All in all, they are a comfortable, dependable, and durable type of rig. Most important of all, their aesthetic value is known and appreciated by every sailor who has romance in his heart. And don't we all?

XXVI

Keeping Ahead of Trouble

With the thought that it might help some other fellow keep out of trouble, somewhere . . . sometime, I'm going to let down my fast-disappearing hair and unburden myself of some opinions and observations regarding the seamier side of sailing—the dangerous situation and how to meet it, the avoidance of trouble, and my own form of mental DDT that kills the butterflies in my stomach.

I have been swamped, capsized and dismasted, and fear was right there with me, my heart pounding like a piledriver and my mouth full of cotton. In fact on some occasions I suppose I was afraid just for the hell of it, from force of habit.

In an earlier chapter I related an experience I had three years ago in which I was hit by a line squall in total darkness, the meanest situation I've had to meet in all my years on the water. Right there, in the first few moments of that blow I found the answer I had sought so long. Now I *knew* what I had been afraid of all those years. It wasn't the sea, the wind or the boat . . . *I was afraid of myself!* Face to face with the very situation I dreaded meeting I was afraid I lacked the ability to lick it.

Now of course I know this was not an earth-shaking discovery, and I shall go on being scared at not-too-frequent (I hope) intervals. But I can truthfully say that ever since that night I've worried less about getting into trouble, the butterflies flap their wings less frantically, and I have gained an immeasurable amount of self-confidence.

The best way I know of keeping ahead of trouble is to anticipate it—to expect it to happen at the worst possible moment and to *be prepared for it*. Being prepared means more than clenching your teeth and glaring defiantly to windward; it means first and foremost that your ship must be *well-found*. Many beginners don't seem to comprehend what "well-found" implies, and because it is a subject on which I am fanatically opinionated I propose to discuss it here in some detail.

A ship is said to be well-found when she is adequately equipped to meet every emergency, within the limits of common sense. She'll have all the tools, gear and material necessary to effect all the repairs that could reasonably be made at sea. She'll carry enough life-saving equipment to cover every person aboard. Her fire fighting equipment will be adequate and *properly* located. She will have more than one pump, and of sufficient capacity to dispose of large quantities of water in a hurry.

But just having this equipment aboard is not enough. It must be maintained constantly in perfect working order, ready for use at a moment's notice and *accessible*.

This means regular, periodic inspection for chafe, wear and corrosion, and as the skipper you must do this yourself. If anything needs repairing or replacing, don't leave your mooring until it has been done. You may only be going out for an hour's sail in full sight of your home port, but within that one hour Old Man Trouble can hit you with everything in the book.

It is impossible to compile a list of specific items of equipment that would cover the needs of all boats, for what is adequate in a 30 foot sloop could hardly apply to a 50 foot schooner. In the smaller craft with its limited stowage space it takes some heavy thinking to decide how much is indispensable, but it is my contention that it is far better to sacrifice a little physical comfort if it is going to mean more *mental* comfort. I haven't met anyone yet who enjoyed being scared.

I like to have plenty of tools on board, particularly woodworking kind. This means a good claw hammer, a couple of chisels, a hacksaw with extra blades, a hand drill with a *complete* set of drills, one or two good files, and a boatbuilder's screw clamp with an 8 inch opening. The last can double as a vise or a large monkey wrench. Some spare pieces of wood are an absolute necessity —a fair sized board or two and a couple of heavy blocks. The boards can be used to fish a spar or nail over a broken plank in the hull, and the blocks will furnish plugs for a broken seacock or through-hull connection.

Caulking tools should be carried at all times—a caulking iron, plenty of cotton and a can of underwater seam compound. Rigging tools I have discussed elsewhere, and it goes without saying that if you have an engine you will also have a decent set of motor tools. Make yourself a ditty box with a tight fitting cover, just big enough to hold your tools, and there'll be less chance of rust getting at them.

Much has been written about fire fighting equipment and its installation and use, generally by experts in that particular field. I am far from being an expert for my experience in that subject has been limited, but I have learned a few things that I have never seen in print. The only extinguishers I have used are the hand-operated carbontetrachloride type. Time and again I have had to throw away an extinguisher within a few months after it was purchased because it was inoperative. Now an extinguisher that won't work is worse than useless because you may discover it just when your life depends on it, so I decided to learn *why* they failed so often. I hacked one apart to have a look at its innards and discovered it was more complicated than I had supposed. Fortunately I had a friend in the business, and from him I learned the whys and wherefores.

Carbontet, as we call it, is in itself corrosive. If you add water to it, it is doubly so. Now unless the extinguisher is *completely* filled, condensation occurs in the air space and corrosion follows rapidly. Corrosion will cause one of two things, or both. The pump will freeze up until it's immovable or the nozzle will be clogged. To keep the extinguisher in working condition you should test it frequently—I do it every 30 days. Pump at least 10 strokes into a clean container—a milk bottle is excellent—and then pour it all back. Never test it without refilling it completely.

The best known manufacturer of this type of extinguisher adds an anti-corrosion agent to the carbontet. Their refill liquid is sold under their trade name, and I have found it to be superior to ordinary carbontet.

The hazards of fire and explosion caused by gasoline are a source of concern to every yachtsman, but the skipper of a small auxiliary must be doubly cautious. Rarely does he have the protection of an elaborate, automatic built-in extinguisher system, and more often than not his motor compartment lacks blowers for venting explosive fumes. Consequently he is perpetually sniffing like a bird dog as he goes about feeling fuel line, carburetor and tank for the telltale wetness that denotes a leak, and he does an almighty amount of worrying about it—which is a darn good habit to have.

When I pull into the gas pump I make sure that no one is smoking, no lamps are lit, and the stove is out. Under no circumstance will I *ever* step on the starter to get under way immediately the deck plate is screwed home. A line of boats may be waiting their turn, but they can curse me and be damned, for I insist on waiting until stray gas fumes have had ample time to dissipate.

On a sultry, oppressive evening some years ago two young lads decided to take a short run in their father's small cruiser to cool off. After opening up the boat, which lay at a bulkhead in a creek, they brought a 5 gallon can of gas from their car and poured it carefully through a funnel into the tank. Not a drop of gas was spilled, and the deck plate was promptly replaced, after which one of the boys carried the empty can and funnel 150 feet away to the car. Upon his return he went below and brought up the kerosene-burning running lights. Standing on the bulkhead by the boat he lit a match, and there followed a terrific flash and explosion that was heard two blocks away. He was blown into the water by the blast and horribly burned. His companion dove overboard and pulled him out, although he himself was likewise burned, and that both are alive today is nothing short of a miracle.

There was no fire—just the initial blast and it was all over. In the combination of still air, high humidity and high temperature, the gasoline vapor released in emptying the can had hung suspended over that boat for an estimated 20 minutes until the match set it off. So gas fumes do *not* have to be confined to explode, and that's why I'm scared when tanking up.

To explain my feelings about bilge pumps I want to relate another incident. About 20 years ago a 45 foot schooner was sailing along the south coast of Long Island bound toward Block Island and points east. Aboard were the owner and his wife, a 17-year-old boy, and an elderly man. Both men had had many years of experience on the water, and for obvious reasons I shall not identify them further.

Nearing Montauk they ran into a severe northeast storm and carried away the mainmast in the middle of the night. Shortly they were under bare poles with the motor going to keep the ship headed into the wind. The motor was in a bulk-headed compartment and could be reached only through a small hatch in the deck. For several hours water had been streaming into this compartment from a bad leak around the stern post, but it wasn't discovered until the water was so high it short-circuited the electrical system, killed the engine and started a fire. Fortunately the fire was easily extinguished.

Now believe it or not, the only bilge pump in that 45 foot schooner was a dinky little electrically driven gadget which at best could squirt a stream hardly bigger than a lead pencil! With this out of commission their only means of getting that water out was with a sponge and a bucket, which had to be passed up through the hatch to be emptied, while the yacht rolled helplessly in the trough of the sea. Somehow they got the water level down to a point where they could get at the leak, and managed to plug it up until it was reduced to a trickle. Meanwhile they had been blown some 60 miles offshore, and providentially they were sighted by a naval vessel which took them off and towed the battered and beaten schooner into port. How a man of experience could put to sea in such an ill-equipped craft I can't understand to this day. To lack so simple a thing as a good hand-operated pump is just asking for trouble in a big way.

Most yachts are equipped with a Navy-type brass pump, generally permanently installed in the cockpit or below deck, and they are quite efficient so long as their intake has the protection of an adequate screen or strainer. But for getting large quantities of water out in a hurry you can't beat the old fashioned galvanized bilge pump, with its wooden handle, leather plunger and leather clapper valve. It throws a man-sized, gushing stream of water that is mighty comforting to behold, and it takes in its stride the hairpins, sand, screws, nuts and burnt matchsticks that can put the Navy-type pump out of business.

For normal, every day use I have one of the Navy-type pumps, and it is quite satisfactory, but since I am determined to keep ahead of trouble insofar as it is possible, I do not consider this one pump at all adequate. Lashed up under the deck in the forepeak is a 3 inch galvanized pump 6 feet long—long enough to reach from the lowest point in the bilge to well above the sill of the cabin companionway. I have never used it and I pray I will never have to, but if I am ever pooped by a king-size sea and find 2 feet of water over the floorboards it's going to be mighty handy. Once a year I break it out and give the leathers a soaking of neatsfoot oil to make sure it is in working order at all times. It is awkward to stow, and it is in the way of the pipe berth, but every time I crack my head on it I remember why it is there and am comforted.

Keeping ahead of trouble calls for eternal vigilance and the use of all the imagination you possess, both in fair weather and foul, but when a cruise involves a fairly long passage in the open sea with no harbor to duck into until you reach your destination, this is doubly true. Here normal routine and procedures no longer suffice and a new set of rules should be adopted. Preparations should be made for every eventuality, and the time to make them is before you start.

First and foremost, in my opinion, is the importance of lashings and stowage. Every movable piece of gear or equipment not required in the operation of the yacht, or that would be needed in an emergency should be stowed below deck. There are some who put the anchor in this category and in this I heartily disagree. How do they *know* they won't be needing the anchor, and possibly in a hurry? I want my *best* anchor and 160 feet of stout cable up on the fore deck, made up and lashed securely with slipped reef knots, ready for use at all times. Running along the coast with a lee shore close at hand has on more than one occasion reminded me of the possibility of drifting or being blown ashore, and I feel a lot better knowing my anchor is right there where I would be needing it.

Lifelines give one a considerable feeling of security and may save a life, for the hazard of falling overboard is very real. Not all cruising yachts have permanent lifelines however, and temporary ones must be rigged. Never mind how they look—any arrangement is better than none at all. On a small sloop, for example, one or two stout lines can be secured to the stemhead fitting, then clove-hitched to each shroud about breast high, and belayed to a cleat or whatever is suitable on the after deck. They may not keep you from going over, but at least there is something to grab as you fall.

The problem of what to do with the dinghy is a controversial one, and its solution depends on two factors: whether it can be taken aboard, and how well it tows. Through my own experience and observation I am convinced that if it is at all possible it should be taken aboard and lashed securely. When the going gets real tough I don't want to have to worry about my tender sheering wildly astern, filling with water or towing under. I carry mine turned over on the port side deck, one gunwale resting in the waterways and the other on the cabin trunk. Two diagonal lashings of several passes keep her from shifting, and should I need to get her overboard in a hurry she could be freed with two swipes of my sheath knife.

I keep at all times a coil of rope within easy reach of the helm. Not any old rope, but a very special rope for a very special purpose. Having witnessed several near-drownings I feel a lot better knowing I have something to heave to a person in the water besides life preservers, and that there is a possibility of hauling him back on board. It is a 65 foot heaving line of 9-thread *new* manila with a *Monkey's Fist* knot in one end, weighted with a wooden ball. It can be thrown with considerable accuracy and the wooden ball keeps it from sinking out of sight.

Life jackets belong in the cockpit, not below deck under the berths. It is surprising how many boats carry them stowed away below in the least accessible place, and some yachtsmen seem to take the attitude that they are carrying them just to comply with the law. I'll admit that they are space eaters, and the smaller the boat the more of a problem they become. On the other hand it is surprising how many can be tucked under a cockpit seat, and as pillows or cushions for taking one's ease in fine weather they can pay their own way. But when the going gets rough or a tight situation develops the best way to dispose of them is to *put them on*.

Along our coasts are numerous inlets, all of them treacherous. Seas make up with astonishing rapidity, channels may shift with every storm and the tidal flow is vicious. Even under the most ideal conditions and with what the charts refer to as "local knowledge," the use of these inlets should not be considered lightly. I have been through Fire Island Inlet on numerous occasions, in sail and in power craft, and each time I was scared. Once I came in after dark on a flood tide and saw a lighted buoy *under water,* and I hardly drew a normal breath until we were safely in.

Now I don't consider myself abnormally timid, but I'll never use one of those inlets unless the wind, sea and tide present ideal conditions, and there are certain precautions I insist on taking. Before approaching the dangerous area I want every person aboard to put on a life jacket. To the unthinking witness I may look silly in a life jacket with a smooth sea and everything under control, but I'd look a damn sight sillier floundering around in the drink *without* one.

I want a capable man up forward as a lookout, and my best anchor made up and ready for him to drop if it should be needed. Since the *Morning Star* is an auxiliary I'll have the sails set and the motor on, for if the motor conks it will happen at the worst possible spot, and under sail alone I'll have steerage way at least. This is one time when I don't want the dinghy on deck—I feel much better towing it up close, on a shortened painter. Finally, I would never attempt a passage in the first place without consulting the nearest Coast Guard Station. Those boys are kept so busy going to the aid of distressed inlet-runners that they have more "local knowledge" than anyone.

But to get back to the subject of the well found ship. For night sailing a good spotlight can often keep you out of trouble. Two or three flashlights are a necessity, but they are of little use when running down the buoys in a strange harbor. Trying to separate the flashers from the neon beer signs and autos running along behind a row of buildings is bad enough, believe me, but if you can't read the numbers on the cans and nuns you are doubly handicapped.

Portable searchlights that clamp on a 7½ volt dry battery throw a beam up to a mile, and they are quite inexpensive. When running a strange channel at night, station a lookout up forward with the portable light, and warn him to sing out to the helmsman when about to flash it, so he may avert his eyes. Night vision is a tricky thing, and if you look directly at a white light you will be practically blind for some time. For the same reason I have a small flashlight with several thicknesses of red cellophane covering the lens, held in place by a rubber band, to use for reading the chart or light list.

In the rigging department I believe it pays to really spread yourself, particularly in the matter of spare cordage. Heavy weather sailing increases your responsibilities and multiplies your worries, for the threat of sudden emergency is very real. Here, at the very time you depend on it most, here is where the turnbuckle snaps, the sheet chafes through or the gooseneck parts its moorings.

A half-dozen wire rope clamps of a size to fit your wire will enable you to jury-rig a shroud or stay if a turnbuckle lets go. Just double the wire back on itself and secure it with 2 or 3 clamps, put a shackle in the chain-plate and set up the shroud with a lanyard. Have a complete assortment of spare shackles, from the smallest made, up to a size to hold your heaviest anchor. Put a small box of assorted brass cotter pins in your ditty box, along with a spool or two of stout wire—brass, copper or annealed stainless steel serving wire. I'm partial to Monel wire—it's not easy to obtain but it will stand a lot more bending without crystallizing. Spare fastenings are often needed, and this means plenty of galvanized nails and brass or bronze wood screws.

I don't believe there's much danger of having too much spare cordage aboard, for most boats seem to suffer from the lack of it. Aside from parted sheets and hal-yards to replace, there are vangs, preventers and lifelines to rig, innumerable seizings and emergency lashings, gaskets and reefing gear. Specific recommendations are not possible, but common sense and an earnest prepara-tion for trouble demand that you have an adequate supply of small stuff and plenty of spare rope. And when I say rope I don't mean a fuzzy, moth eaten sec-tion of a worn-out main sheet—I mean *new* rope, with the ends whipped. I hate to be aboard a nice yacht and find her rope locker filled with a nondescript collection of long-deceased rope. It's downright unseamanlike and a mark of incompetence.

In conclusion, let it be said that if a careful study of this book affords the reader even half as much pleasure as learning the arts of the sailor has afforded the author, he will have succeeded in his purpose. You may rest assured that the practice of these arts will do more than provide pleasure; it will help you keep ahead of trouble and encourage the practice of sound seamanship.

Index

A CATALOG OF SELECTED
DOVER BOOKS
IN ALL FIELDS OF INTEREST

A CATALOG OF SELECTED DOVER
BOOKS IN ALL FIELDS OF INTEREST

CONCERNING THE SPIRITUAL IN ART, Wassily Kandinsky. Pioneering work by father of abstract art. Thoughts on color theory, nature of art. Analysis of earlier masters. 12 illustrations. 80pp. of text. 5⅜ x 8½.   23411-8 Pa. $3.95

ANIMALS: 1,419 Copyright-Free Illustrations of Mammals, Birds, Fish, Insects, etc., Jim Harter (ed.). Clear wood engravings present, in extremely lifelike poses, over 1,000 species of animals. One of the most extensive pictorial sourcebooks of its kind. Captions. Index. 284pp. 9 x 12.   23766-4 Pa. $12.95

CELTIC ART: The Methods of Construction, George Bain. Simple geometric techniques for making Celtic interlacements, spirals, Kells-type initials, animals, humans, etc. Over 500 illustrations. 160pp. 9 x 12. (USO)   22923-8 Pa. $9.95

AN ATLAS OF ANATOMY FOR ARTISTS, Fritz Schider. Most thorough reference work on art anatomy in the world. Hundreds of illustrations, including selections from works by Vesalius, Leonardo, Goya, Ingres, Michelangelo, others. 593 illustrations. 192pp. 7⅛ x 10¼.   20241-0 Pa. $9 95

CELTIC HAND STROKE-BY-STROKE (Irish Half-Uncial from "The Book of Kells"): An Arthur Baker Calligraphy Manual, Arthur Baker. Complete guide to creating each letter of the alphabet in distinctive Celtic manner. Covers hand position, strokes, pens, inks, paper, more. Illustrated. 48pp. 8¼ x 11.   24336-2 Pa. $3.95

EASY ORIGAMI, John Montroll. Charming collection of 32 projects (hat, cup, pelican, piano, swan, many more) specially designed for the novice origami hobbyist. Clearly illustrated easy-to-follow instructions insure that even beginning papercrafters will achieve successful results. 48pp. 8¼ x 11.   27298-2 Pa. $2.95

THE COMPLETE BOOK OF BIRDHOUSE CONSTRUCTION FOR WOOD-WORKERS, Scott D. Campbell. Detailed instructions, illustrations, tables. Also data on bird habitat and instinct patterns. Bibliography. 3 tables. 63 illustrations in 15 figures. 48pp. 5¼ x 8½.   24407-5 Pa. $2.50

BLOOMINGDALE'S ILLUSTRATED 1886 CATALOG: Fashions, Dry Goods and Housewares, Bloomingdale Brothers. Famed merchants' extremely rare catalog depicting about 1,700 products: clothing, housewares, firearms, dry goods, jewelry, more. Invaluable for dating, identifying vintage items. Also, copyright-free graphics for artists, designers. Co-published with Henry Ford Museum & Greenfield Village. 160pp. 8¼ x 11.   25780-0 Pa. $9.95

HISTORIC COSTUME IN PICTURES, Braun & Schneider. Over 1,450 costumed figures in clearly detailed engravings—from dawn of civilization to end of 19th century. Captions. Many folk costumes. 256pp. 8⅜ x 11¾.   23150-X Pa. $12.95

CATALOG OF DOVER BOOKS

STICKLEY CRAFTSMAN FURNITURE CATALOGS, Gustav Stickley and L. & J. G. Stickley. Beautiful, functional furniture in two authentic catalogs from 1910. 594 illustrations, including 277 photos, show settles, rockers, armchairs, reclining chairs, bookcases, desks, tables. 183pp. 6½ x 9¼. 23838-5 Pa. $9.95

AMERICAN LOCOMOTIVES IN HISTORIC PHOTOGRAPHS: 1858 to 1949, Ron Ziel (ed.). A rare collection of 126 meticulously detailed official photographs, called "builder portraits," of American locomotives that majestically chronicle the rise of steam locomotive power in America. Introduction. Detailed captions. xi + 129pp. 9 x 12. 27393-8 Pa. $12.95

AMERICA'S LIGHTHOUSES: An Illustrated History, Francis Ross Holland, Jr. Delightfully written, profusely illustrated fact-filled survey of over 200 American lighthouses since 1716. History, anecdotes, technological advances, more. 240pp. 8 x 10¾. 25576-X Pa. $12.95

TOWARDS A NEW ARCHITECTURE, Le Corbusier. Pioneering manifesto by founder of "International School." Technical and aesthetic theories, views of industry, economics, relation of form to function, "mass-production split" and much more. Profusely illustrated. 320pp. 6⅛ x 9¼. (USO) 25023-7 Pa. $9.95

HOW THE OTHER HALF LIVES, Jacob Riis. Famous journalistic record, exposing poverty and degradation of New York slums around 1900, by major social reformer. 100 striking and influential photographs. 233pp. 10 x 7⅞. 22012-5 Pa. $10.95

FRUIT KEY AND TWIG KEY TO TREES AND SHRUBS, William M. Harlow. One of the handiest and most widely used identification aids. Fruit key covers 120 deciduous and evergreen species; twig key 160 deciduous species. Easily used. Over 300 photographs. 126pp. 5⅜ x 8½. 20511-8 Pa. $3.95

COMMON BIRD SONGS, Dr. Donald J. Borror. Songs of 60 most common U.S. birds: robins, sparrows, cardinals, bluejays, finches, more—arranged in order of increasing complexity. Up to 9 variations of songs of each species.
Cassette and manual 99911-4 $8.95

ORCHIDS AS HOUSE PLANTS, Rebecca Tyson Northen. Grow cattleyas and many other kinds of orchids—in a window, in a case, or under artificial light. 63 illustrations. 148pp. 5⅜ x 8½. 23261-1 Pa. $4.95

MONSTER MAZES, Dave Phillips. Masterful mazes at four levels of difficulty. Avoid deadly perils and evil creatures to find magical treasures. Solutions for all 32 exciting illustrated puzzles. 48pp. 8¼ x 11. 26005-4 Pa. $2.95

MOZART'S DON GIOVANNI (DOVER OPERA LIBRETTO SERIES), Wolfgang Amadeus Mozart. Introduced and translated by Ellen H. Bleiler. Standard Italian libretto, with complete English translation. Convenient and thoroughly portable—an ideal companion for reading along with a recording or the performance itself. Introduction. List of characters. Plot summary. 121pp. 5¼ x 8½. 24944-1 Pa. $2.95

TECHNICAL MANUAL AND DICTIONARY OF CLASSICAL BALLET, Gail Grant. Defines, explains, comments on steps, movements, poses and concepts. 15-page pictorial section. Basic book for student, viewer. 127pp. 5⅜ x 8½. 21843-0 Pa. $4.95

BRASS INSTRUMENTS: Their History and Development, Anthony Baines. Authoritative, updated survey of the evolution of trumpets, trombones, bugles, cornets, French horns, tubas and other brass wind instruments. Over 140 illustrations and 48 music examples. Corrected and updated by author. New preface. Bibliography. 320pp. 5⅜ x 8½. 27574-4 Pa. $9.95

HOLLYWOOD GLAMOR PORTRAITS, John Kobal (ed.). 145 photos from 1926-49. Harlow, Gable, Bogart, Bacall; 94 stars in all. Full background on photographers, technical aspects. 160pp. 8⅜ x 11¼. 23352-9 Pa. $11.95

MAX AND MORITZ, Wilhelm Busch. Great humor classic in both German and English. Also 10 other works: "Cat and Mouse," "Plisch and Plumm," etc. 216pp. 5⅜ x 8½. 20181-3 Pa. $6.95

THE RAVEN AND OTHER FAVORITE POEMS, Edgar Allan Poe. Over 40 of the author's most memorable poems: "The Bells," "Ulalume," "Israfel," "To Helen," "The Conqueror Worm," "Eldorado," "Annabel Lee," many more. Alphabetic lists of titles and first lines. 64pp. 5³⁄₁₆ x 8¼. 26685-0 Pa. $1.00

PERSONAL MEMOIRS OF U. S. GRANT, Ulysses Simpson Grant. Intelligent, deeply moving firsthand account of Civil War campaigns, considered by many the finest military memoirs ever written. Includes letters, historic photographs, maps and more. 528pp. 6⅛ x 9¼. 28587-1 Pa. $11.95

AMULETS AND SUPERSTITIONS, E. A. Wallis Budge. Comprehensive discourse on origin, powers of amulets in many ancient cultures: Arab, Persian Babylonian, Assyrian, Egyptian, Gnostic, Hebrew, Phoenician, Syriac, etc. Covers cross, swastika, crucifix, seals, rings, stones, etc. 584pp. 5⅜ x 8½. 23573-4 Pa. $12.95

RUSSIAN STORIES/PYCCKNE PACCKA3bI: A Dual-Language Book, edited by Gleb Struve. Twelve tales by such masters as Chekhov, Tolstoy, Dostoevsky, Pushkin, others. Excellent word-for-word English translations on facing pages, plus teaching and study aids, Russian/English vocabulary, biographical/critical introductions, more. 416pp. 5⅜ x 8½. 26244-8 Pa. $8.95

PHILADELPHIA THEN AND NOW: 60 Sites Photographed in the Past and Present, Kenneth Finkel and Susan Oyama. Rare photographs of City Hall, Logan Square, Independence Hall, Betsy Ross House, other landmarks juxtaposed with contemporary views. Captures changing face of historic city. Introduction. Captions. 128pp. 8¼ x 11. 25790-8 Pa. $9.95

AIA ARCHITECTURAL GUIDE TO NASSAU AND SUFFOLK COUNTIES, LONG ISLAND, The American Institute of Architects, Long Island Chapter, and the Society for the Preservation of Long Island Antiquities. Comprehensive, well-researched and generously illustrated volume brings to life over three centuries of Long Island's great architectural heritage. More than 240 photographs with authoritative, extensively detailed captions. 176pp. 8¼ x 11. 26946-9 Pa. $14.95

NORTH AMERICAN INDIAN LIFE: Customs and Traditions of 23 Tribes, Elsie Clews Parsons (ed.). 27 fictionalized essays by noted anthropologists examine religion, customs, government, additional facets of life among the Winnebago, Crow, Zuni, Eskimo, other tribes. 480pp. 6⅛ x 9¼. 27377-6 Pa. $10.95

FRANK LLOYD WRIGHT'S HOLLYHOCK HOUSE, Donald Hoffmann. Lavishly illustrated, carefully documented study of one of Wright's most controversial residential designs. Over 120 photographs, floor plans, elevations, etc. Detailed perceptive text by noted Wright scholar. Index. 128pp. 9¼ x 10¾. 27133-1 Pa. $11.95

THE MALE AND FEMALE FIGURE IN MOTION: 60 Classic Photographic Sequences, Eadweard Muybridge. 60 true-action photographs of men and women walking, running, climbing, bending, turning, etc., reproduced from rare 19th-century masterpiece. vi + 121pp. 9 x 12. 24745-7 Pa. $10.95

1001 QUESTIONS ANSWERED ABOUT THE SEASHORE, N. J. Berrill and Jacquelyn Berrill. Queries answered about dolphins, sea snails, sponges, starfish, fishes, shore birds, many others. Covers appearance, breeding, growth, feeding, much more. 305pp. 5¼ x 8¼. 23366-9 Pa. $8.95

GUIDE TO OWL WATCHING IN NORTH AMERICA, Donald S. Heintzelman. Superb guide offers complete data and descriptions of 19 species: barn owl, screech owl, snowy owl, many more. Expert coverage of owl-watching equipment, conservation, migrations and invasions, etc. Guide to observing sites. 84 illustrations. xiii + 193pp. 5⅜ x 8½. 27344-X Pa. $8.95

MEDICINAL AND OTHER USES OF NORTH AMERICAN PLANTS: A Historical Survey with Special Reference to the Eastern Indian Tribes, Charlotte Erichsen-Brown. Chronological historical citations document 500 years of usage of plants, trees, shrubs native to eastern Canada, northeastern U.S. Also complete identifying information. 343 illustrations. 544pp. 6½ x 9¼. 25951-X Pa. $12.95

STORYBOOK MAZES, Dave Phillips. 23 stories and mazes on two-page spreads: Wizard of Oz, Treasure Island, Robin Hood, etc. Solutions. 64pp. 8¼ x 11. 23628-5 Pa. $2.95

NEGRO FOLK MUSIC, U.S.A., Harold Courlander. Noted folklorist's scholarly yet readable analysis of rich and varied musical tradition. Includes authentic versions of over 40 folk songs. Valuable bibliography and discography. xi + 324pp. 5⅜ x 8½. 27350-4 Pa. $7.95

MOVIE-STAR PORTRAITS OF THE FORTIES, John Kobal (ed.). 163 glamor, studio photos of 106 stars of the 1940s: Rita Hayworth, Ava Gardner, Marlon Brando, Clark Gable, many more. 176pp. 8⅜ x 11¼. 23546-7 Pa. $12.95

BENCHLEY LOST AND FOUND, Robert Benchley. Finest humor from early 30s, about pet peeves, child psychologists, post office and others. Mostly unavailable elsewhere. 73 illustrations by Peter Arno and others. 183pp. 5⅜ x 8½. 22410-4 Pa. $6.95

YEKL and THE IMPORTED BRIDEGROOM AND OTHER STORIES OF YIDDISH NEW YORK, Abraham Cahan. Film Hester Street based on Yekl (1896). Novel, other stories among first about Jewish immigrants on N.Y.'s East Side. 240pp. 5⅜ x 8½. 22427-9 Pa. $6.95

SELECTED POEMS, Walt Whitman. Generous sampling from *Leaves of Grass*. Twenty-four poems include "I Hear America Singing," "Song of the Open Road," "I Sing the Body Electric," "When Lilacs Last in the Dooryard Bloom'd," "O Captain! My Captain!"—all reprinted from an authoritative edition. Lists of titles and first lines. 128pp. 5³⁄₁₆ x 8¼. 26878-0 Pa. $1.00

THE BEST TALES OF HOFFMANN, E. T. A. Hoffmann. 10 of Hoffmann's most important stories: "Nutcracker and the King of Mice," "The Golden Flowerpot," etc. 458pp. 5⅜ x 8½. 21793-0 Pa. $9.95

FROM FETISH TO GOD IN ANCIENT EGYPT, E. A. Wallis Budge. Rich detailed survey of Egyptian conception of "God" and gods, magic, cult of animals, Osiris, more. Also, superb English translations of hymns and legends. 240 illustrations. 545pp. 5⅜ x 8½. 25803-3 Pa. $11.95

FRENCH STORIES/CONTES FRANÇAIS: A Dual-Language Book, Wallace Fowlie. Ten stories by French masters, Voltaire to Camus: "Micromegas" by Voltaire; "The Atheist's Mass" by Balzac; "Minuet" by de Maupassant; "The Guest" by Camus, six more. Excellent English translations on facing pages. Also French-English vocabulary list, exercises, more. 352pp. 5⅜ x 8½. 26443-2 Pa. $8.95

CHICAGO AT THE TURN OF THE CENTURY IN PHOTOGRAPHS: 122 Historic Views from the Collections of the Chicago Historical Society, Larry A. Viskochil. Rare large-format prints offer detailed views of City Hall, State Street, the Loop, Hull House, Union Station, many other landmarks, circa 1904-1913. Introduction. Captions. Maps. 144pp. 9⅜ x 12¼. 24656-6 Pa. $12.95

OLD BROOKLYN IN EARLY PHOTOGRAPHS, 1865-1929, William Lee Younger. Luna Park, Gravesend race track, construction of Grand Army Plaza, moving of Hotel Brighton, etc. 157 previously unpublished photographs. 165pp. 8⅞ x 11¾. 23587-4 Pa. $13.95

THE MYTHS OF THE NORTH AMERICAN INDIANS, Lewis Spence. Rich anthology of the myths and legends of the Algonquins, Iroquois, Pawnees and Sioux, prefaced by an extensive historical and ethnological commentary. 36 illustrations. 480pp. 5⅜ x 8½. 25967-6 Pa. $8.95

AN ENCYCLOPEDIA OF BATTLES: Accounts of Over 1,560 Battles from 1479 B.C. to the Present, David Eggenberger. Essential details of every major battle in recorded history from the first battle of Megiddo in 1479 B.C. to Grenada in 1984. List of Battle Maps. New Appendix covering the years 1967-1984. Index. 99 illustrations. 544pp. 6½ x 9¼. 24913-1 Pa. $14.95

SAILING ALONE AROUND THE WORLD, Captain Joshua Slocum. First man to sail around the world, alone, in small boat. One of great feats of seamanship told in delightful manner. 67 illustrations. 294pp. 5⅜ x 8½. 20326-3 Pa. $5.95

ANARCHISM AND OTHER ESSAYS, Emma Goldman. Powerful, penetrating, prophetic essays on direct action, role of minorities, prison reform, puritan hypocrisy, violence, etc. 271pp. 5⅜ x 8½. 22484-8 Pa. $6.95

MYTHS OF THE HINDUS AND BUDDHISTS, Ananda K. Coomaraswamy and Sister Nivedita. Great stories of the epics; deeds of Krishna, Shiva, taken from puranas, Vedas, folk tales; etc. 32 illustrations. 400pp. 5⅜ x 8½. 21759-0 Pa. $10.95

BEYOND PSYCHOLOGY, Otto Rank. Fear of death, desire of immortality, nature of sexuality, social organization, creativity, according to Rankian system. 291pp. 5⅜ x 8½. 20485-5 Pa. $8.95

A THEOLOGICO-POLITICAL TREATISE, Benedict Spinoza. Also contains unfinished Political Treatise. Great classic on religious liberty, theory of government on common consent. R. Elwes translation. Total of 421pp. 5⅜ x 8½. 20249-6 Pa. $9.95

MY BONDAGE AND MY FREEDOM, Frederick Douglass. Born a slave, Douglass became outspoken force in antislavery movement. The best of Douglass' autobiographies. Graphic description of slave life. 464pp. 5⅜ x 8½. 22457-0 Pa. $8.95

FOLLOWING THE EQUATOR: A Journey Around the World, Mark Twain. Fascinating humorous account of 1897 voyage to Hawaii, Australia, India, New Zealand, etc. Ironic, bemused reports on peoples, customs, climate, flora and fauna, politics, much more. 197 illustrations. 720pp. 5⅜ x 8½. 26113-1 Pa. $15.95

THE PEOPLE CALLED SHAKERS, Edward D. Andrews. Definitive study of Shakers: origins, beliefs, practices, dances, social organization, furniture and crafts, etc. 33 illustrations. 351pp. 5⅜ x 8½. 21081-2 Pa. $8.95

THE MYTHS OF GREECE AND ROME, H. A. Guerber. A classic of mythology, generously illustrated, long prized for its simple, graphic, accurate retelling of the principal myths of Greece and Rome, and for its commentary on their origins and significance. With 64 illustrations by Michelangelo, Raphael, Titian, Rubens, Canova, Bernini and others. 480pp. 5⅜ x 8½. 27584-1 Pa. $9.95

PSYCHOLOGY OF MUSIC, Carl E. Seashore. Classic work discusses music as a medium from psychological viewpoint. Clear treatment of physical acoustics, auditory apparatus, sound perception, development of musical skills, nature of musical feeling, host of other topics. 88 figures. 408pp. 5⅜ x 8½. 21851-1 Pa. $10.95

THE PHILOSOPHY OF HISTORY, Georg W. Hegel. Great classic of Western thought develops concept that history is not chance but rational process, the evolution of freedom. 457pp. 5⅜ x 8½. 20112-0 Pa. $9.95

THE BOOK OF TEA, Kakuzo Okakura. Minor classic of the Orient: entertaining, charming explanation, interpretation of traditional Japanese culture in terms of tea ceremony. 94pp. 5⅜ x 8½. 20070-1 Pa. $3.95

LIFE IN ANCIENT EGYPT, Adolf Erman. Fullest, most thorough, detailed older account with much not in more recent books, domestic life, religion, magic, medicine, commerce, much more. Many illustrations reproduce tomb paintings, carvings, hieroglyphs, etc. 597pp. 5⅜ x 8½. 22632-8 Pa. $11.95

SUNDIALS, Their Theory and Construction, Albert Waugh. Far and away the best, most thorough coverage of ideas, mathematics concerned, types, construction, adjusting anywhere. Simple, nontechnical treatment allows even children to build several of these dials. Over 100 illustrations. 230pp. 5⅜ x 8½. 22947-5 Pa. $7.95

DYNAMICS OF FLUIDS IN POROUS MEDIA, Jacob Bear. For advanced students of ground water hydrology, soil mechanics and physics, drainage and irrigation engineering, and more. 335 illustrations. Exercises, with answers. 784pp. 6⅛ x 9¼. 65675-6 Pa. $19.95

SONGS OF EXPERIENCE: Facsimile Reproduction with 26 Plates in Full Color, William Blake. 26 full-color plates from a rare 1826 edition. Includes "The Tyger," "London," "Holy Thursday," and other poems. Printed text of poems. 48pp. 5¼ x 7. 24636-1 Pa. $4.95

OLD-TIME VIGNETTES IN FULL COLOR, Carol Belanger Grafton (ed.). Over 390 charming, often sentimental illustrations, selected from archives of Victorian graphics—pretty women posing, children playing, food, flowers, kittens and puppies, smiling cherubs, birds and butterflies, much more. All copyright-free. 48pp. 9¼ x 12¼. 27269-9 Pa. $5.95

PERSPECTIVE FOR ARTISTS, Rex Vicat Cole. Depth, perspective of sky and sea, shadows, much more, not usually covered. 391 diagrams, 81 reproductions of drawings and paintings. 279pp. 5⅜ x 8½. 22487-2 Pa. $6.95

DRAWING THE LIVING FIGURE, Joseph Sheppard. Innovative approach to artistic anatomy focuses on specifics of surface anatomy, rather than muscles and bones. Over 170 drawings of live models in front, back and side views, and in widely varying poses. Accompanying diagrams. 177 illustrations. Introduction. Index. 144pp. 8⅜ x11¼. 26723-7 Pa. $8.95

GOTHIC AND OLD ENGLISH ALPHABETS: 100 Complete Fonts, Dan X. Solo. Add power, elegance to posters, signs, other graphics with 100 stunning copyright-free alphabets: Blackstone, Dolbey, Germania, 97 more–including many lower-case, numerals, punctuation marks. 104pp. 8⅛ x 11. 24695-7 Pa. $8.95

HOW TO DO BEADWORK, Mary White. Fundamental book on craft from simple projects to five-bead chains and woven works. 106 illustrations. 142pp. 5⅜ x 8. 20697-1 Pa. $4.95

THE BOOK OF WOOD CARVING, Charles Marshall Sayers. Finest book for beginners discusses fundamentals and offers 34 designs. "Absolutely first rate . . . well thought out and well executed."–E. J. Tangerman. 118pp. 7¾ x 10⅝. 23654-4 Pa. $6.95

ILLUSTRATED CATALOG OF CIVIL WAR MILITARY GOODS: Union Army Weapons, Insignia, Uniform Accessories, and Other Equipment, Schuyler, Hartley, and Graham. Rare, profusely illustrated 1846 catalog includes Union Army uniform and dress regulations, arms and ammunition, coats, insignia, flags, swords, rifles, etc. 226 illustrations. 160pp. 9 x 12. 24939-5 Pa. $10.95

WOMEN'S FASHIONS OF THE EARLY 1900s: An Unabridged Republication of "New York Fashions, 1909," National Cloak & Suit Co. Rare catalog of mail-order fashions documents women's and children's clothing styles shortly after the turn of the century. Captions offer full descriptions, prices. Invaluable resource for fashion, costume historians. Approximately 725 illustrations. 128pp. 8⅜ x 11¼. 27276-1 Pa. $11.95

THE 1912 AND 1915 GUSTAV STICKLEY FURNITURE CATALOGS, Gustav Stickley. With over 200 detailed illustrations and descriptions, these two catalogs are essential reading and reference materials and identification guides for Stickley furniture. Captions cite materials, dimensions and prices. 112pp. 6½ x 9¼. 26676-1 Pa. $9.95

EARLY AMERICAN LOCOMOTIVES, John H. White, Jr. Finest locomotive engravings from early 19th century: historical (1804–74), main-line (after 1870), special, foreign, etc. 147 plates. 142pp. 11⅜ x 8¼. 22772-3 Pa. $10.95

THE TALL SHIPS OF TODAY IN PHOTOGRAPHS, Frank O. Braynard. Lavishly illustrated tribute to nearly 100 majestic contemporary sailing vessels: Amerigo Vespucci, Clearwater, Constitution, Eagle, Mayflower, Sea Cloud, Victory, many more. Authoritative captions provide statistics, background on each ship. 190 black-and-white photographs and illustrations. Introduction. 128pp. 8⅞ x 11¾. 27163-3 Pa. $13.95

CATALOG OF DOVER BOOKS

EARLY NINETEENTH-CENTURY CRAFTS AND TRADES, Peter Stockham (ed.). Extremely rare 1807 volume describes to youngsters the crafts and trades of the day: brickmaker, weaver, dressmaker, bookbinder, ropemaker, saddler, many more. Quaint prose, charming illustrations for each craft. 20 black-and-white line illustrations. 192pp. 4⅝ x 6. 27293-1 Pa. $4.95

VICTORIAN FASHIONS AND COSTUMES FROM HARPER'S BAZAR, 1867–1898, Stella Blum (ed.). Day costumes, evening wear, sports clothes, shoes, hats, other accessories in over 1,000 detailed engravings. 320pp. 9⅜ x 12¼. 22990-4 Pa. $14.95

GUSTAV STICKLEY, THE CRAFTSMAN, Mary Ann Smith. Superb study surveys broad scope of Stickley's achievement, especially in architecture. Design philosophy, rise and fall of the Craftsman empire, descriptions and floor plans for many Craftsman houses, more. 86 black-and-white halftones. 31 line illustrations. Introduction 208pp. 6½ x 9¼. 27210-9 Pa. $9.95

THE LONG ISLAND RAIL ROAD IN EARLY PHOTOGRAPHS, Ron Ziel. Over 220 rare photos, informative text document origin (1844) and development of rail service on Long Island. Vintage views of early trains, locomotives, stations, passengers, crews, much more. Captions. 8⅞ x 11¾. 26301-0 Pa. $13.95

THE BOOK OF OLD SHIPS: From Egyptian Galleys to Clipper Ships, Henry B. Culver. Superb, authoritative history of sailing vessels, with 80 magnificent line illustrations. Galley, bark, caravel, longship, whaler, many more. Detailed, informative text on each vessel by noted naval historian. Introduction. 256pp. 5⅜ x 8½. 27332-6 Pa. $7.95

TEN BOOKS ON ARCHITECTURE, Vitruvius. The most important book ever written on architecture. Early Roman aesthetics, technology, classical orders, site selection, all other aspects. Morgan translation. 331pp. 5⅜ x 8½. 20645-9 Pa. $8.95

THE HUMAN FIGURE IN MOTION, Eadweard Muybridge. More than 4,500 stopped-action photos, in action series, showing undraped men, women, children jumping, lying down, throwing, sitting, wrestling, carrying, etc. 390pp. 7⅞ x 10⅝. 20204-6 Clothbd. $25.95

TREES OF THE EASTERN AND CENTRAL UNITED STATES AND CANADA, William M. Harlow. Best one-volume guide to 140 trees. Full descriptions, woodlore, range, etc. Over 600 illustrations. Handy size. 288pp. 4½ x 6⅜. 20395-6 Pa. $5.95

SONGS OF WESTERN BIRDS, Dr. Donald J. Borror. Complete song and call repertoire of 60 western species, including flycatchers, juncoes, cactus wrens, many more–includes fully illustrated booklet. Cassette and manual 99913-0 $8.95

GROWING AND USING HERBS AND SPICES, Milo Miloradovich. Versatile handbook provides all the information needed for cultivation and use of all the herbs and spices available in North America. 4 illustrations. Index. Glossary. 236pp. 5⅜ x 8½. 25058-X Pa. $6.95

BIG BOOK OF MAZES AND LABYRINTHS, Walter Shepherd. 50 mazes and labyrinths in all–classical, solid, ripple, and more–in one great volume. Perfect inexpensive puzzler for clever youngsters. Full solutions. 112pp. 8⅛ x 11. 22951-3 Pa. $4.95

PHOTOGRAPHIC SKETCHBOOK OF THE CIVIL WAR, Alexander Gardner. 100 photos taken on field during the Civil War. Famous shots of Manassas Harper's Ferry, Lincoln, Richmond, slave pens, etc. 244pp. 10⅝ x 8¼.   22731-6 Pa. $9.95

FIVE ACRES AND INDEPENDENCE, Maurice G. Kains. Great back-to-the-land classic explains basics of self-sufficient farming. The one book to get. 95 illustrations. 397pp. 5⅜ x 8½.   20974-1 Pa. $7.95

SONGS OF EASTERN BIRDS, Dr. Donald J. Borror. Songs and calls of 60 species most common to eastern U.S.: warblers, woodpeckers, flycatchers, thrushes, larks, many more in high-quality recording.   Cassette and manual 99912-2 $8.95

A MODERN HERBAL, Margaret Grieve. Much the fullest, most exact, most useful compilation of herbal material. Gigantic alphabetical encyclopedia, from aconite to zedoary, gives botanical information, medical properties, folklore, economic uses, much else. Indispensable to serious reader. 161 illustrations. 888pp. 6½ x 9¼. 2-vol. set. (USO)   Vol. I: 22798-7 Pa. $9.95
Vol. II: 22799-5 Pa. $9.95

HIDDEN TREASURE MAZE BOOK, Dave Phillips. Solve 34 challenging mazes accompanied by heroic tales of adventure. Evil dragons, people-eating plants, blood-thirsty giants, many more dangerous adversaries lurk at every twist and turn. 34 mazes, stories, solutions. 48pp. 8¼ x 11.   24566-7 Pa. $2.95

LETTERS OF W. A. MOZART, Wolfgang A. Mozart. Remarkable letters show bawdy wit, humor, imagination, musical insights, contemporary musical world; includes some letters from Leopold Mozart. 276pp. 5⅜ x 8½.   22859-2 Pa. $7.95

BASIC PRINCIPLES OF CLASSICAL BALLET, Agrippina Vaganova. Great Russian theoretician, teacher explains methods for teaching classical ballet. 118 illustrations. 175pp. 5⅜ x 8½.   22036-2 Pa. $5.95

THE JUMPING FROG, Mark Twain. Revenge edition. The original story of The Celebrated Jumping Frog of Calaveras County, a hapless French translation, and Twain's hilarious "retranslation" from the French. 12 illustrations. 66pp. 5⅜ x 8½.
22686-7 Pa. $3.95

BEST REMEMBERED POEMS, Martin Gardner (ed.). The 126 poems in this superb collection of 19th- and 20th-century British and American verse range from Shelley's "To a Skylark" to the impassioned "Renascence" of Edna St. Vincent Millay and to Edward Lear's whimsical "The Owl and the Pussycat." 224pp. 5⅜ x 8½.
27165-X Pa. $4.95

COMPLETE SONNETS, William Shakespeare. Over 150 exquisite poems deal with love, friendship, the tyranny of time, beauty's evanescence, death and other themes in language of remarkable power, precision and beauty. Glossary of archaic terms. 80pp. 5³⁄₁₆ x 8¼.   26686-9 Pa. $1.00

BODIES IN A BOOKSHOP, R. T. Campbell. Challenging mystery of blackmail and murder with ingenious plot and superbly drawn characters. In the best tradition of British suspense fiction. 192pp. 5⅜ x 8½.   24720-1 Pa. $6.95

THE INFLUENCE OF SEA POWER UPON HISTORY, 1660–1783, A. T. Mahan. Influential classic of naval history and tactics still used as text in war colleges. First paperback edition. 4 maps. 24 battle plans. 640pp. 5⅜ x 8½. 25509-3 Pa. $12.95

THE STORY OF THE TITANIC AS TOLD BY ITS SURVIVORS, Jack Winocour (ed.). What it was really like. Panic, despair, shocking inefficiency, and a little heroism. More thrilling than any fictional account. 26 illustrations. 320pp. 5⅜ x 8½. 20610-6 Pa. $8.95

FAIRY AND FOLK TALES OF THE IRISH PEASANTRY, William Butler Yeats (ed.). Treasury of 64 tales from the twilight world of Celtic myth and legend: "The Soul Cages," "The Kildare Pooka," "King O'Toole and his Goose," many more. Introduction and Notes by W. B. Yeats. 352pp. 5⅜ x 8½. 26941-8 Pa. $8.95

BUDDHIST MAHAYANA TEXTS, E. B. Cowell and Others (eds.). Superb, accurate translations of basic documents in Mahayana Buddhism, highly important in history of religions. The Buddha-karita of Asvaghosha, Larger Sukhavativyuha, more. 448pp. 5⅜ x 8½. 25552-2 Pa. $9.95

ONE TWO THREE . . . INFINITY: Facts and Speculations of Science, George Gamow. Great physicist's fascinating, readable overview of contemporary science: number theory, relativity, fourth dimension, entropy, genes, atomic structure, much more. 128 illustrations. Index. 352pp. 5⅜ x 8½. 25664-2 Pa. $8.95

ENGINEERING IN HISTORY, Richard Shelton Kirby, et al. Broad, nontechnical survey of history's major technological advances: birth of Greek science, industrial revolution, electricity and applied science, 20th-century automation, much more. 181 illustrations. ". . . excellent . . ."–*Isis*. Bibliography. vii + 530pp. 5⅜ x 8¼. 26412-2 Pa. $14.95

DALÍ ON MODERN ART: The Cuckolds of Antiquated Modern Art, Salvador Dalí. Influential painter skewers modern art and its practitioners. Outrageous evaluations of Picasso, Cézanne, Turner, more. 15 renderings of paintings discussed. 44 calligraphic decorations by Dalí. 96pp. 5⅜ x 8½. (USO) 29220-7 Pa. $4.95

ANTIQUE PLAYING CARDS: A Pictorial History, Henry René D'Allemagne. Over 900 elaborate, decorative images from rare playing cards (14th–20th centuries): Bacchus, death, dancing dogs, hunting scenes, royal coats of arms, players cheating, much more. 96pp. 9¼ x 12¼. 29265-7 Pa. $11.95

MAKING FURNITURE MASTERPIECES: 30 Projects with Measured Drawings, Franklin H. Gottshall. Step-by-step instructions, illustrations for constructing handsome, useful pieces, among them a Sheraton desk, Chippendale chair, Spanish desk, Queen Anne table and a William and Mary dressing mirror. 224pp. 8⅛ x 11¼. 29338-6 Pa. $13.95

THE FOSSIL BOOK: A Record of Prehistoric Life, Patricia V. Rich et al. Profusely illustrated definitive guide covers everything from single-celled organisms and dinosaurs to birds and mammals and the interplay between climate and man. Over 1,500 illustrations. 760pp. 7½ x 10⅛. 29371-8 Pa. $29.95

Prices subject to change without notice.

Available at your book dealer or write for free catalog to Dept. GI, Dover Publications, Inc., 31 East 2nd St., Mineola, N.Y. 11501. Dover publishes more than 500 books each year on science, elementary and advanced mathematics, biology, music, art, literary history, social sciences and other areas.